# KING*f*ISHER

# First
# Picture Atlas

KING*f*ISHER

KINGFISHER
Kingfisher Publications Plc
New Penderel House, 283-288 High Holborn, London WC1V 7HZ
www.kingfisherpub.com

First published in hardback 1994
First published in paperback 1998
Copyright © Kingfisher Publications Plc 1994
3 5 7 9 10 8 6 4 2

A CIP catalogue record for this book is available from the British Library

ISBN 0 7534 0268 8 (pb)

1PREM/0108/TWP/P&W(cover/MAR)/130SMA

0 7534 0296 3 (hb)

Typeset by Tradespool Ltd, Frome, Somerset
Colour separation by P & W Graphics, Singapore
Printed in Singapore

# Contents

# About this Atlas

Most of the world's land is divided up into seven large continents. In this atlas, six of the continents are shown twice. The first map shows all of the independent countries within each continent. (An independent country is one with its own government.) And the second map shows the major rivers, lakes and mountains. The seventh continent, Antarctica, has just one map. This is because there are no people living there all year round.

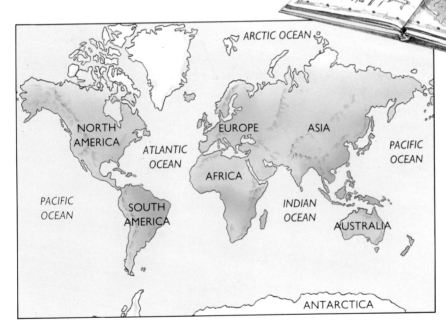

## About the maps

On the first maps each country is clearly marked in a separate colour with its capital city. The second maps are picture maps. They show the kind of animals that live on each continent, some of the plants that grow there, and the main industries. It is not possible, however, to show every spot where, for example, tigers or factories are found. There will be tigers and factories in other places besides those marked.

On the maps you will see where the biggest mountain ranges are, where the rivers flow to, what the names of the largest lakes are, as well as the names of the countries and their capital cities.

Each map has a scale. This will help you to work out how large the continent really is.

| 0 | 200 | 400 | 600 | 800 kilometres |
| 0 | 100 | 200 | 300 | 400 | 500 miles |

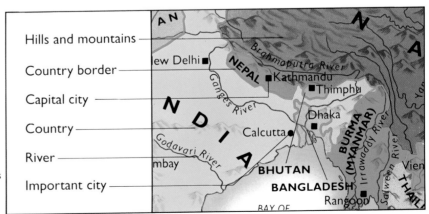

- Hills and mountains
- Country border
- Capital city
- Country
- River
- Important city

## Where is it?

If you want to find a particular place in the atlas, look for it first in the index. After the place name you will see a page number and then a number and a letter, such as **4C**. This is the grid reference. Remember it as you turn to the page. Now look for the grid number (in a red circle) at the top and bottom of the page. There is a faint blue line running on either side of them, up and down the page. Now look for the letter, on the left and right-hand sides of the page and the lines running beside these. You will find the place you are looking for in the square where the lines meet.

## MAKING A MEAL OF IT

On the picture-map pages there is a box showing a typical meal from that continent, using the food that is grown there. Of course, people eat a huge variety of things in the different parts of any continent. None the less, each continent does have its own, individual kinds of food, and its own traditional recipes based on the common ingredients that are found in the region.

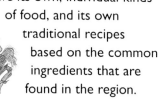

## ANSWER THAT!

On all the map pages there is a box called 'Answer That!' This asks you three questions about the map. You should be able to answer each of the questions by studying the map carefully. Look hard, and you are sure to find the solution – but some questions may require more looking than others! The correct answers to all the questions are given on page 38. Can you think of other questions to ask?

## Where it comes from and where it is made

The picture maps include a series of symbols showing you the main products and industries of a region.

A factory marks an **industry** or industrial area, and logs mark the **logging industry**. An oil rig shows where **oil** is drilled, and a flame shows **gas** production.

A mining trolley full of coal or metal, and two gemstones show where **mining** takes place.

An umbrella and suitcase show that the **tourist industry** is important in that area.

Large-scale **fishing** is represented by a trawler, and **animal farming** by two bullocks (for beef cattle), a dairy cow, a sheep and a pig.

Maize, an ear of wheat and a rice plant show where these important **cereals** are widely grown.

Various kinds of **fruit farming** are important in many parts of the world. These are shown by apples and pears, oranges and lemons, bananas, and grapes (which are also used to make wine).

**Tea, coffee and cocoa** are important and valuable crops. These are shown by tea leaves, coffee beans and cocoa pods.

**Palm trees** provide other crops such as copra from coconut palms (used to make coconut oil), dates from date palms and palm oil.

**Groundnuts** are better known as peanuts, and **sugar cane** is used to make sugar. Natural **rubber** is harvested from trees, and **cotton** comes from the fluffy seedheads of the cotton plant.

 Factory

 Logging

 Oil

 Gas

 Mining

 Gemstones

 Tourism

 Fishing

 Beef cattle

 Dairy cows

 Sheep

 Pigs

 Maize

 Wheat

 Rice

 Apples and pears

 Citrus fruits

 Bananas

 Grapes and wine

 Tea

 Coffee

 Cocoa

 Palm tree

 Groundnuts

 Sugar cane

 Rubber

  Cotton

# How maps are made

Maps are very clear and simple pictures of the world. They show us where places are, and how we might get from one place to another. Maps of the world are the result of years of work by navigators and surveyors, who have visited the places and measured the shapes of land, the heights of mountains, the courses of rivers and the position of towns and cities. In recent years, pictures from space have helped to make maps even more accurate.

One of the big problems with maps of the world is that the world is not flat, but round.

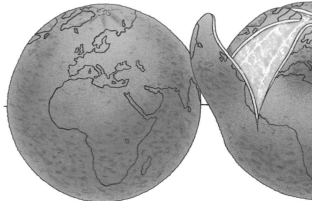

To draw a flat map of the round world we have to cheat a little. Imagine the world as an orange.

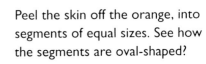

Peel the skin off the orange, into segments of equal sizes. See how the segments are oval-shaped?

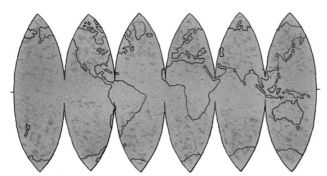

With the whole peel removed you have a true picture of the surface of the world divided into a row of oval segments.

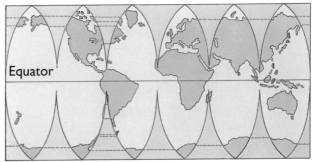

But this does not make a very helpful map. So we cheat by stretching the Earth's surface to fill in the gaps between the segments to make a rectangle.

## Map and scales

**1.** Using scale is a way of drawing places very much smaller than they are in real life, but still showing exactly where they are. If you are in Paris you can see the Eiffel Tower at its real size.

**2.** A map of the Eiffel Tower will need to be drawn smaller than real size – to a smaller scale. So, for example, every 2 centimetres on the map is equal to 150 metres of the real place or area.

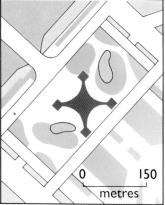

**3.** Maps can be drawn to any scale depending on what they are trying to show. A map of Paris shows the area of the city and two sizes of roads, but cannot show the Eiffel Tower in detail.

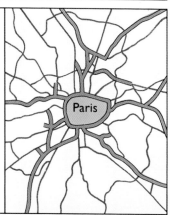

**4.** With an even smaller scale, a map will show much less detail about the city itself, but more about the country around it. A map of France will simply show where Paris is placed in the country.

## Make your own map

Try making your own map of a place you know well, such as the area between your home and your school. Imagine how it would look from above. Draw in the streets, and show where all the main buildings are. Add any railways, parks, rivers and bridges. Keep the map as simple as possible by using symbols so that you can get more information into a small space. Could your friends use the map to find your home?

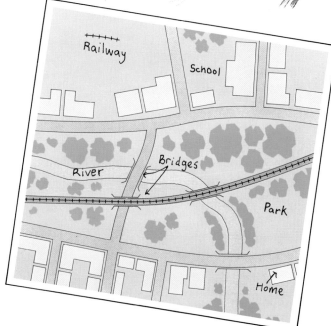

# Climate and lands

Every part of the world has its own climate or pattern of weather. It may be warm in summer, rainy in spring and very cold in winter. Or it may be hot all year round. The climate of a country depends on the shape of its land, as well as its position in the world.

| | |
|---|---|
| | Polar |
| | Cool and snowy |
| | Temperate |
| | Dry land and desert |
| | Tropical |
| | Mountain |

**This map of the world** shows where the six main types of climate are found. Each climate is shown in a different colour.

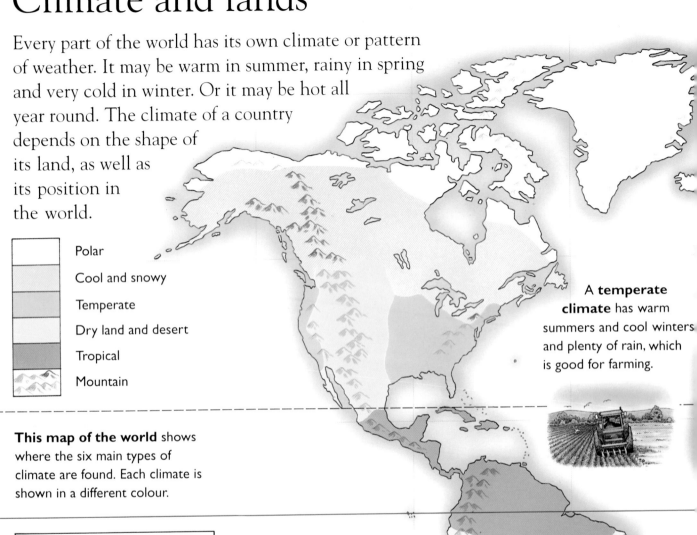

A **temperate climate** has warm summers and cool winters and plenty of rain, which is good for farming.

**SOME WORLD FACTS**
**Longest river** the Nile River (6,670 kilometres).
**Highest mountain** Mount Everest (8,848 metres).
**Highest waterfall** Angel Falls, Venezuela 979 metres.
**Largest country** Russia (17 million square kilometres).
**Smallest independent country** the Vatican City State, in Italy (less that half a square kilometre).
**Largest continent** Asia.
**Smallest continent** Australia.
**Largest ocean** the Pacific.

The world can be divided into two halves by an imaginary line called the Equator. The Tropics form a band around the Equator between two more imaginary lines called the Tropic of Cancer and the Tropic of Capricorn. The Tropics receive the heat of the Sun from directly overhead. A **tropical climate** is hot and there is plenty of rain.

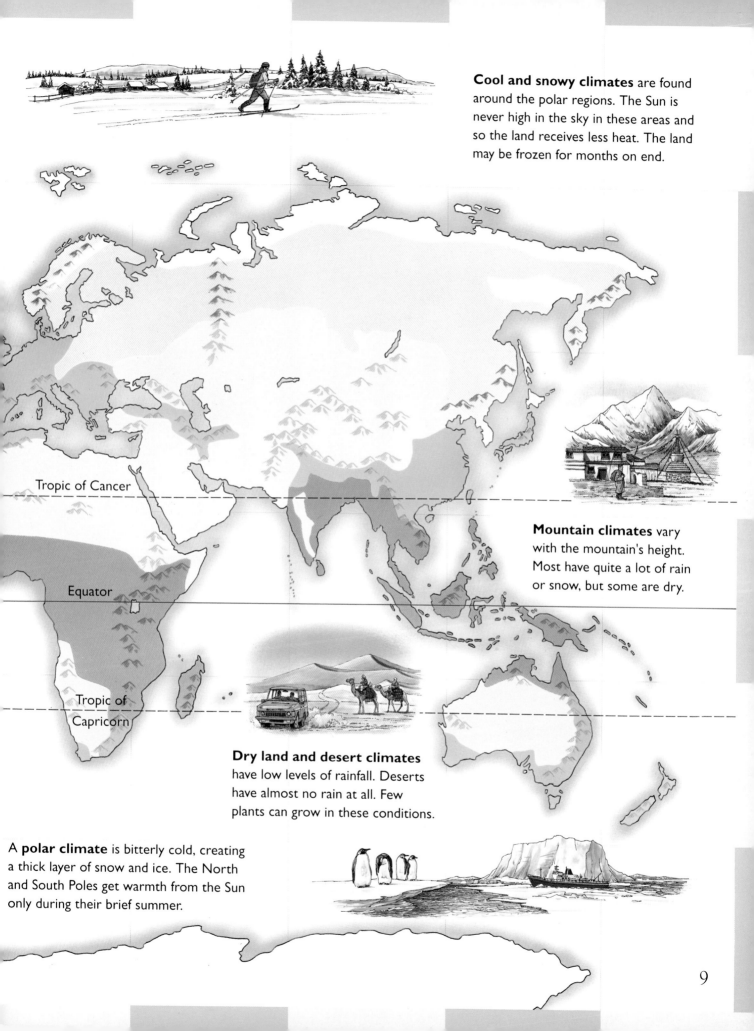

**Cool and snowy climates** are found around the polar regions. The Sun is never high in the sky in these areas and so the land receives less heat. The land may be frozen for months on end.

Tropic of Cancer

**Mountain climates** vary with the mountain's height. Most have quite a lot of rain or snow, but some are dry.

Equator

Tropic of Capricorn

**Dry land and desert climates** have low levels of rainfall. Deserts have almost no rain at all. Few plants can grow in these conditions.

A **polar climate** is bitterly cold, creating a thick layer of snow and ice. The North and South Poles get warmth from the Sun only during their brief summer.

# North America

Two English-speaking countries occupy most of North America: Canada and the United States of America (or USA). The USA is one of the world's richest and most powerful countries. It is divided into 50 states, including the huge, separate state of Alaska.

To the south lies the warm Caribbean Sea, with hundreds of islands. A ribbon of land links North America to South America and contains a cluster of Spanish-speaking countries. Together these are known as Central America.

**The Inuit (or Eskimo) people** live in the very cold lands in the far north of Canada. In the past, they made houses called igloos from blocks of snow, and travelled on dog-sleds. Now they also use motorized snowmobiles.

kilometres
0   400   800   1200   1600

miles
0   200   400   600   800   1000

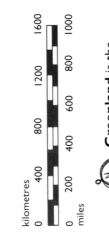

**Greenland** is the largest island in the world. Although it is close to North America, its government is linked to Denmark. Most of the land is covered with snow and ice.

**Greenland (Denmark)**

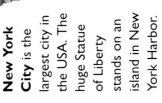

**New York City** is the largest city in the USA. The huge Statue of Liberty stands on an island in New York Harbor.

**St Pierre et Miquelon (France)**

ARCTIC OCEAN

ATLANTIC OCEAN

PACIFIC OCEAN

INDIAN OCEAN

HUDSON BAY

*Mackenzie River*

*Yukon River*

*Saskatchewan River*

**Alaska (USA)**

C A N A D A

**Canada** is the second largest country in the world. The northern part is remote and empty. Most people live in the south, close to the USA.

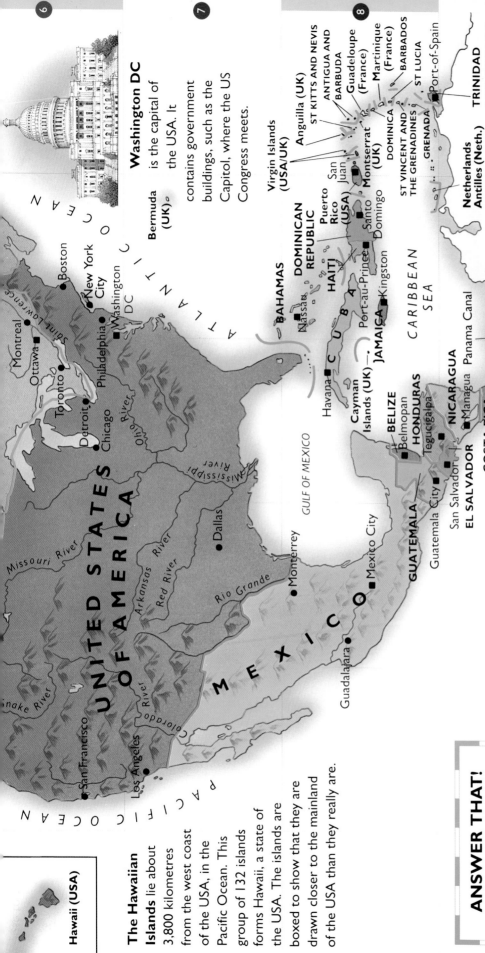

## Washington DC

is the capital of the USA. It contains government buildings, such as where the US Congress meets.

**Hawaii (USA)**

**The Hawaiian Islands** lie about 3,800 kilometres from the west coast of the USA, in the Pacific Ocean. This group of 132 islands forms Hawaii, a state of the USA. The islands are boxed to show that they are drawn closer to the mainland of the USA than they really are.

**ATLANTIC OCEAN**

Bermuda (UK)

Boston
New York City
Washington DC
Philadelphia

Montreal
Ottawa
Toronto
Detroit
Chicago
Saint Lawrence River

**UNITED STATES OF AMERICA**

Missouri River
Snake River
Colorado River
Arkansas River
Red River
Ohio River
MISSISSIPPI River

San Francisco
Los Angeles
Dallas

**PACIFIC OCEAN**

Rio Grande
Monterrey
Mexico City
Guadalajara

**M E X I C O**

GULF OF MEXICO

Havana
**C U B A**
Cayman Islands (UK)
**BAHAMAS**
Nassau
**JAMAICA**
Kingston
**HAITI**
Port-au-Prince
**DOMINICAN REPUBLIC**
Santo Domingo
San Juan
**Puerto Rico (USA)**
Virgin Islands (USA/UK)
Anguilla (UK)
**ST KITTS AND NEVIS**
**ANTIGUA AND BARBUDA**
**Guadeloupe (France)**
**Montserrat (UK)**
**DOMINICA**
**Martinique (France)**
**ST LUCIA**
**BARBADOS**
**ST VINCENT AND THE GRENADINES**
**GRENADA**
Port-of-Spain
**TRINIDAD AND TOBAGO**

**CARIBBEAN SEA**

**BELIZE**
Belmopan
**GUATEMALA**
Guatemala City
**HONDURAS**
Tegucigalpa
**EL SALVADOR**
San Salvador
**NICARAGUA**
Managua
**COSTA RICA**
San José
**PANAMA**
Panama City
Panama Canal

**Netherlands Antilles (Neth.)**

For the capital cities of the smaller islands, look up the country name in the index.

## St Kitts and Nevis

are two small Caribbean islands, which together form the smallest independent country in North America.

### The Panama Canal

was opened in 1914. Before then, ships had to sail all the way round South America to travel between the Pacific and the Atlantic Oceans.

**Mexico** is a Spanish-speaking country with volcanoes and mountains, and long, sandy beaches. Its capital, Mexico City, is one of the largest cities in the world.

## ANSWER THAT!

1. Which country is attached to the south of the USA?

2. Which is the largest island in the Caribbean Sea?

3. Which island is called green, but is hardly green at all?

11

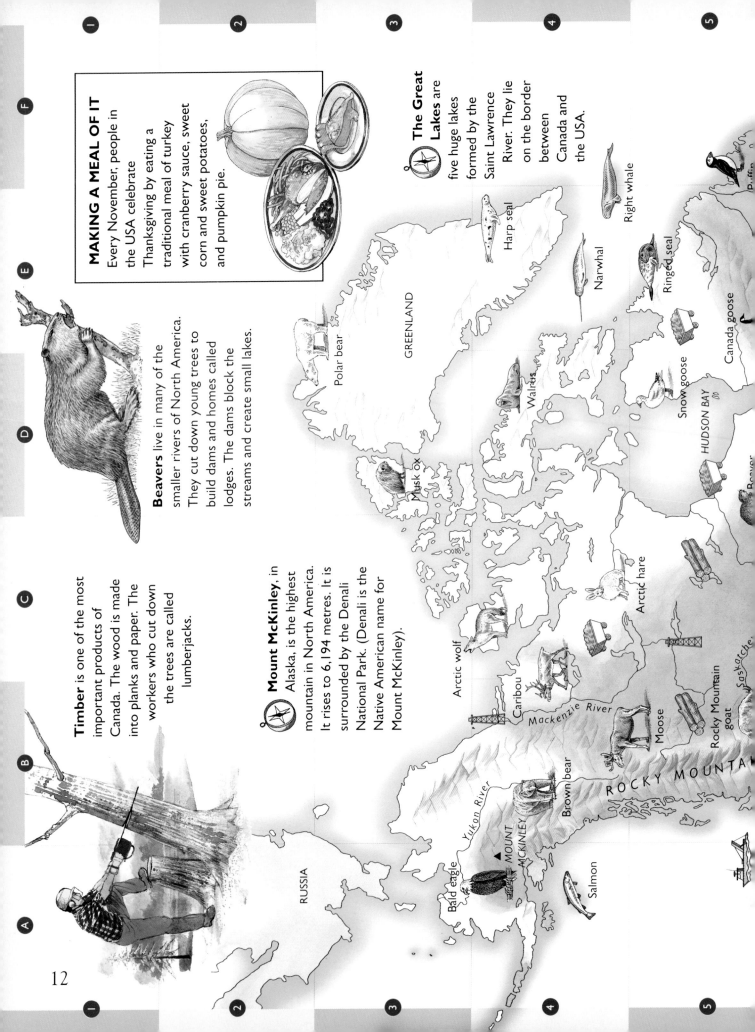

## MAKING A MEAL OF IT

Every November, people in the USA celebrate Thanksgiving by eating a traditional meal of turkey with cranberry sauce, sweet corn and sweet potatoes, and pumpkin pie.

**The Great Lakes** are five huge lakes formed by the Saint Lawrence River. They lie on the border between Canada and the USA.

**Beavers** live in many of the smaller rivers of North America. They cut down young trees to build dams and homes called lodges. The dams block the streams and create small lakes.

**Timber** is one of the most important products of Canada. The wood is made into planks and paper. The workers who cut down the trees are called lumberjacks.

**Mount McKinley,** in Alaska, is the highest mountain in North America. It rises to 6,194 metres. It is surrounded by the Denali National Park. (Denali is the Native American name for Mount McKinley).

Harp seal

Right whale

Narwhal

Ringed seal

GREENLAND

Canada goose

Walrus

Snow goose

Polar bear

Musk ox

HUDSON BAY

Puffin

Beaver

Arctic hare

Arctic wolf

Caribou

Mackenzie River

Moose

Rocky Mountain goat

Saskatche...

RUSSIA

Bald eagle

▲ MOUNT McKINLEY

Yukon River

Brown bear

ROCKY MOUNTA...

Salmon

12

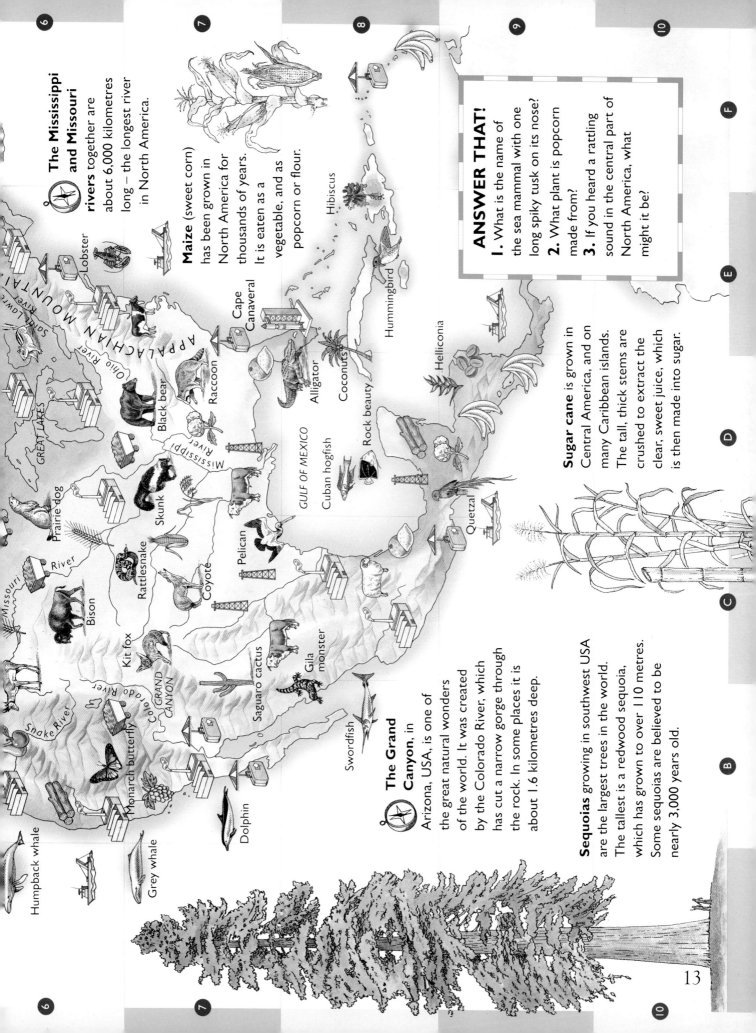

**The Mississippi and Missouri rivers** together are about 6,000 kilometres long – the longest river in North America.

**Maize** (sweet corn) has been grown in North America for thousands of years. It is eaten as a vegetable, and as popcorn or flour.

## ANSWER THAT!

1. What is the name of the sea mammal with one long spiky tusk on its nose?
2. What plant is popcorn made from?
3. If you heard a rattling sound in the central part of North America, what might it be?

**Sugar cane** is grown in Central America, and on many Caribbean islands. The tall, thick stems are crushed to extract the clear, sweet juice, which is then made into sugar.

**The Grand Canyon**, in Arizona, USA, is one of the great natural wonders of the world. It was created by the Colorado River, which has cut a narrow gorge through the rock. In some places it is about 1.6 kilometres deep.

**Sequoias** growing in southwest USA are the largest trees in the world. The tallest is a redwood sequoia, which has grown to over 110 metres. Some sequoias are believed to be nearly 3,000 years old.

Hibiscus
Cape Canaveral
Hummingbird
Helliconia
Lobster
Black bear
Raccoon
Alligator
Coconuts
Rock beauty
GULF OF MEXICO
Cuban hogfish
Quetzal
GREAT LAKES
Ohio River
Saint Lawrence River
APPALACHIAN MOUNTAINS
Mississippi River
Prairie dog
Skunk
Rattlesnake
Pelican
Coyote
Missouri River
Bison
Kit fox
GRAND CANYON
Colorado River
Snake River
Gila monster
Saguaro cactus
Monarch butterfly
Swordfish
Dolphin
Humpback whale
Grey whale

13

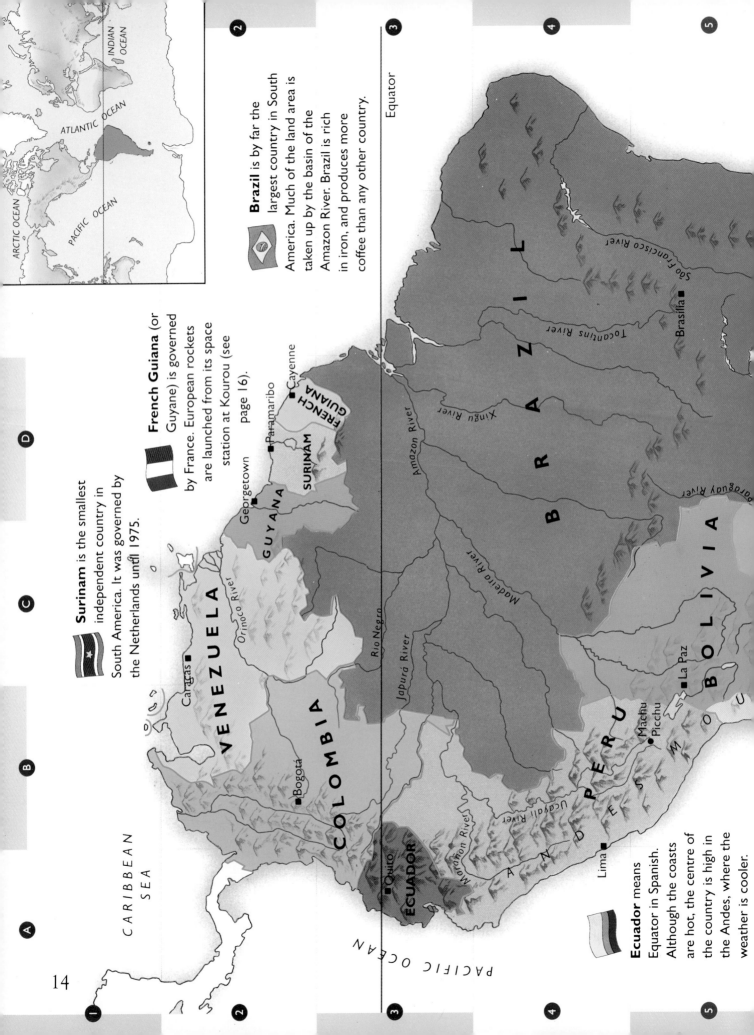

14

ARCTIC OCEAN

ATLANTIC OCEAN

PACIFIC OCEAN

INDIAN OCEAN

**Surinam** is the smallest independent country in South America. It was governed by the Netherlands until 1975.

**French Guiana** (or Guyane) is governed by France. European rockets are launched from its space station at Kourou (see page 16).

**Brazil** is by far the largest country in South America. Much of the land area is taken up by the basin of the Amazon River. Brazil is rich in iron, and produces more coffee than any other country.

**Ecuador** means Equator in Spanish. Although the coasts are hot, the centre of the country is high in the Andes, where the weather is cooler.

Equator

CARIBBEAN SEA

VENEZUELA
Caracas ■

COLOMBIA
Bogotá ■

GUYANA
Georgetown ■

SURINAM
Paramaribo ■

FRENCH GUIANA
Cayenne ■

Orinoco River

Rio Negra

Japurá River

Amazon River

Marañon River

Ucayali River

Madeira River

Xingu River

Tocantins River

São Francisco River

Paraguay River

ECUADOR
Quito ■

PERU
Lima ■
Machu Picchu ●

BOLIVIA
La Paz ■

A N D E S   M O U N T A

B R A Z I L

Brasília ■

PACIFIC OCEAN

Equator

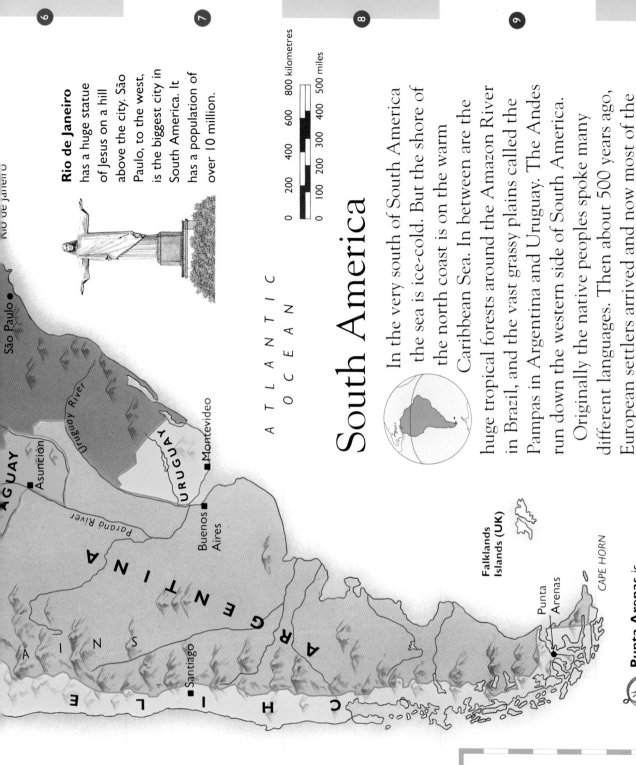

# South America

In the very south of South America the sea is ice-cold. But the shore of the north coast is on the warm Caribbean Sea. In between are the huge tropical forests around the Amazon River in Brazil, and the vast grassy plains called the Pampas in Argentina and Uruguay. The Andes run down the western side of South America. Originally the native peoples spoke many different languages. Then about 500 years ago, European settlers arrived and now most of the people of South America speak Spanish, except in Brazil, where the main language is Portuguese.

**Rio de Janeiro** has a huge statue of Jesus on a hill above the city. São Paulo, to the west, is the biggest city in South America. It has a population of over 10 million.

ATLANTIC OCEAN

Uruguay River
Paraná River
São Paulo
Asunción
Montevideo
Buenos Aires
Santiago
URUGUAY
ARGENTINA
CHILE
ANDES
Falklands Islands (UK)
Punta Arenas
CAPE HORN

0  200  400  600  800 kilometres
0  100  200  300  400  500 miles

**La Paz** is the world's highest capital city, standing 3,627 metres above sea level. The air is thinner at this height, and visitors from other lower countries can feel quite breathless.

**Machu Picchu** is a ruined city of the ancient Inca people. It lies high in the mountains of Peru and remained hidden for hundreds of years before it was rediscovered in 1911.

**Punta Arenas** is further south than any other city in the world.

## ANSWER THAT!

1. How many countries in South America begin with the letter B?
2. What is the name of the longest and thinnest country in South America?
3. Which country has coasts on the Pacific Ocean and on the Caribbean Sea?

16

**The Angel Falls** is the highest waterfall in the world. The water tumbles from a height of 979 metres.

CARIBBEAN SEA

Giant leatherback turtle

Kourou

ANDES

PACIFIC OCEAN

Orinoco River

Macaw

ANGEL FALLS

Surinam toad

GUIANA HIGHLANDS

Manatee

Amazon River

Sloth

Piranha

Kapok tree

Rio Negro

Japurá River

Harpy eagle

Brazil nut tree

Anaconda

Xingu River

Madeira River

Capybara

Poison arrow frog

Marañon River

Ucayali River

Llama

LAKE TITICACA

Spider Monkey

Marmoset

Tarantula

Toucan

Tocantins River

Kinkajou

Hummingbird

Giant anteater

São Francisco River

Tapir

Howler monkey

**ANSWER THAT!**

**1.** Which South American animal likes to hang upside down from branches?

**2.** One animal likes to eat ants, which it picks up with its sticky tongue. What is its name?

**3.** Which frog can be used to make poison arrows?

**Cocoa** is grown in the warm parts of South America. Chocolate is made from the seeds, or beans, that are found inside the cocoa pods.

**The Amazon River** is 6,448 kilometres long (slightly shorter than the Nile River in Africa). However, it carries far more water than any other river in the world, and 60 times more than the Nile.

**Lake Titicaca** is the largest freshwater lake in South America. It is 3,812 metres above sea level. The ferry service across the lake is the world's highest.

**Football** is a favourite sport all over South America. Brazil was the first country to win the World Cup three times.

**The Pampas** covers much of Argentina and Uruguay. Large herds of beef cattle are raised on these huge grassy plains. They are looked after by cowboys called gauchos.

## MAKING A MEAL OF IT

Many of our common foods come originally from South America. These include sweet corn, tomatoes and potatoes. A common meal in South America consists of beef, served with boiled rice or potatoes, tomatoes and slices of fried plantain (a fruit like a banana).

**Elephant seals** are the largest of all seals. They live in cold waters and breed on the shores of southern Argentina. Male elephant seals can be as much as 6 metres long.

The **Atacama Desert** is one of the driest places on Earth. Some parts of it have gone 400 years without rain.

**Condors** are large vultures that live in the Andes. Some have a wingspan of over 3.2 metres. They feed on the bodies of dead animals.

**The Andes** form the longest mountain range in the world. They stretch for over 7,250 kilometres. The highest peak is Aconcagua, which rises to 6,959 metres.

ATLANTIC OCEAN

Jaguar

Uruguay River

Paraná River

Par

Guinea pig

Rhea

Vicuña

ACONCAGUA

Chinchilla

ATACAMA DESERT

Monkey puzzle tree

Armadillo

Patagonian hare

Elephant seal

Fur seal

Magellan penguin

CAPE HORN

Blue whale

17

A

# Europe

There are more than 40 countries in Europe, and about as many languages. This is a wealthy part of the world with many old, historic cities and lots of big industries producing cars, chemicals, medicines and so on. It generally has mild weather, with plenty of rain, which is good for farming. The south of Europe, around the Mediterranean Sea, has very warm summers, while the north is cooler with long, cold and dark winters.

B

Reykjavik **ICELAND**

For the capital cities of the smallest countries, look up the country name in the index.

**Faeroe Islands (Denmark)**

C

**Brussels** is the capital of Belgium. It is also the headquarters of the European Union (or EU). There are 12 nations in the EU: Belgium, Denmark, France, Germany, Greece, Ireland, Italy, Luxembourg, the Netherlands, Portugal, Spain and the UK.

**Paris** is the capital of France and one of the largest cities in Europe. Its many famous buildings include the Eiffel Tower, a huge metal tower built in 1889.

D

| 0 | 200 | 400 | 600 | 800 kilometres |
| 0 | 100 | 200 | 300 | 400 | 500 miles |

E

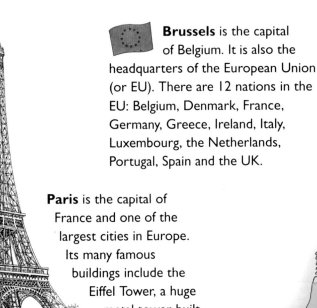

ATLANTIC OCEAN

**REPUBLIC OF IRELAND**   Dublin

**UNITED KINGDOM**   NORTH S

**NETHERLAND**

London   Amste
Rh

ENGLISH CHANNEL   **BELGIUM**

**LUXEMBOURG**   Brussels
Paris   Luxemb

Loire River

BAY OF BISCAY

**FRANCE**

Rhône River

**SWITZERL.**

**ANDORRA**

Po

**MONACO**

**PORTUGAL**   **SPAIN**

Ebro River

Lisbon   Tajo River   Madrid

Barcelona   Co
(Fra

Sard
(Ita

Gibraltar (UK)

MEDITERRANEAN SE

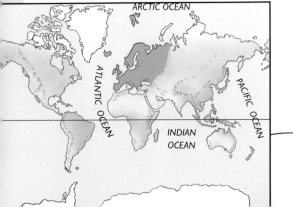

ARCTIC OCEAN

ATLANTIC OCEAN

PACIFIC OCEAN

INDIAN OCEAN

**The Vatican City State** is the smallest country in the world. It lies inside the city of Rome. The Vatican is the headquarters of the Roman Catholic Church, which is led by the Pope.

NORWEGIAN SEA

## ANSWER THAT!
**1.** Which country earned its name because it is so icy? (Clue: it is an island).
**2.** Which city in which country is in both Europe and Asia?
**3.** Which country in Europe begins with the letter C, but does not have any sea around its borders?

NORWAY

SWEDEN

FINLAND

R U S S I A

N. Dvina River

Oslo

Stockholm

Helsinki

St Petersburg

Tallinn

**ESTONIA**

BALTIC SEA

DENMARK

Copenhagen

Riga

**LATVIA**

**LITHUANIA**

Vilnius

Moscow

Ural River

Kaliningrad (Russia)

Minsk

B E L A R U S

Berlin

P O L A N D

GERMANY

Warsaw

Don River

Volga River

Prague

**CZECH REPUBLIC**

U K R A I N E

River

Kiev

**SLOVAKIA**

Vienna

Bratislava

Budapest

**AUSTRIA**

LIECHTENSTEIN

**HUNGARY**

MOLDOVA

Dnepr River

CASPIAN SEA

Ljubljana

Zagreb

R O M A N I A

Chisinau

SLOVENIA

CROATIA

YUGOSLAVIA

SAN MARINO

Sarajevo

Belgrade

Bucharest

BLACK SEA

VATICAN STATE

**BOSNIA-HERZEGOVINA**

Sofia

B U L G A R I A

ITALY

Tirana

Skopje

Istanbul

**ALBANIA**

**MACEDONIA**

G R E E C E

**TURKEY**

**Istanbul** is the largest city in Turkey. Most of Turkey is in Asia, but a small part of it is in Europe. Istanbul lies in both Europe and Asia.

Sicily (Italy)

Valletta

MALTA

Athens

Crete (Greece)

**Moscow** is the capital of Russia, and one of the largest cities in Europe. St Basil's Cathedral is so colourful that it looks as though it might be made of candy – but it is not!

A   B   C   D   E   F

## MAKING A MEAL OF IT

One of the most famous dishes of Europe is pasta from Italy. Pasta is made of wheat flour. Spaghetti and ravioli are types of pasta. Ravioli consists of small pasta envelopes filled with meat or cheese. It is often eaten with a tomato sauce, and sprinkled with grated Parmesan cheese.

**Cork** comes from the thick bark of trees called cork oaks. Portugal is the world's largest producer of cork. Much of it is used to make corks for wine bottles.

**Great Britain** is the largest island in Europe. Other countries this far north have cold climates, but Britain is kept warm by an ocean current of warm water called the Gulf Stream.

**Wild boars** are a kind of wild pig. They are found in many countries of Europe, including Spain and Germany.

Arctic tern

Sperm whale

Icelandic pony

Puffin

Lynx

Wolverine

Red deer

Cormorant

Salmon

Sole

Barn owl

Shamrock

Red squirrel

Rabbit

Badger

Hedgehog

Lobster

Chamois

Fox

Ibex

Marmot

Lammergeier

White stork

Golden eagle

Sardine

Barbary ape

KJOLEN MOUNTAINS

NORTH SEA

BALTIC

ATLANTIC OCEAN

Elbe River

Rhine River

Loire River

Rhone River

Po River

ALPS

PYRENEES

Ebro River

Tajo River

CORSICA

SARDINIA

SICILY

MEDITERRANEAN

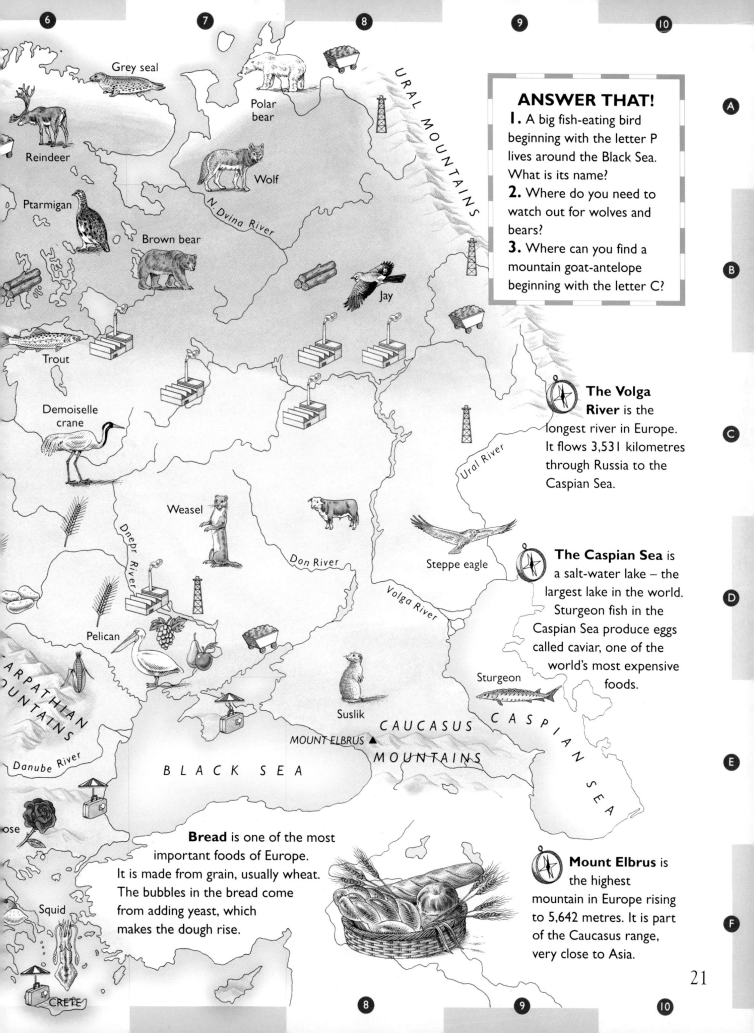

Grey seal

Polar bear

Reindeer

Wolf

N. Dvina River

Ptarmigan

Brown bear

URAL MOUNTAINS

Jay

**ANSWER THAT!**
**1.** A big fish-eating bird beginning with the letter P lives around the Black Sea. What is its name?
**2.** Where do you need to watch out for wolves and bears?
**3.** Where can you find a mountain goat-antelope beginning with the letter C?

Trout

Demoiselle crane

**The Volga River** is the longest river in Europe. It flows 3,531 kilometres through Russia to the Caspian Sea.

Ural River

Weasel

Steppe eagle

Dnepr River

Don River

**The Caspian Sea** is a salt-water lake – the largest lake in the world. Sturgeon fish in the Caspian Sea produce eggs called caviar, one of the world's most expensive foods.

Volga River

Pelican

Sturgeon

CARPATHIAN MOUNTAINS

Suslik

CAUCASUS

CASPIAN SEA

Danube River

MOUNT ELBRUS ▲

MOUNTAINS

BLACK SEA

ose

**Bread** is one of the most important foods of Europe. It is made from grain, usually wheat. The bubbles in the bread come from adding yeast, which makes the dough rise.

Squid

**Mount Elbrus** is the highest mountain in Europe rising to 5,642 metres. It is part of the Caucasus range, very close to Asia.

CRETE

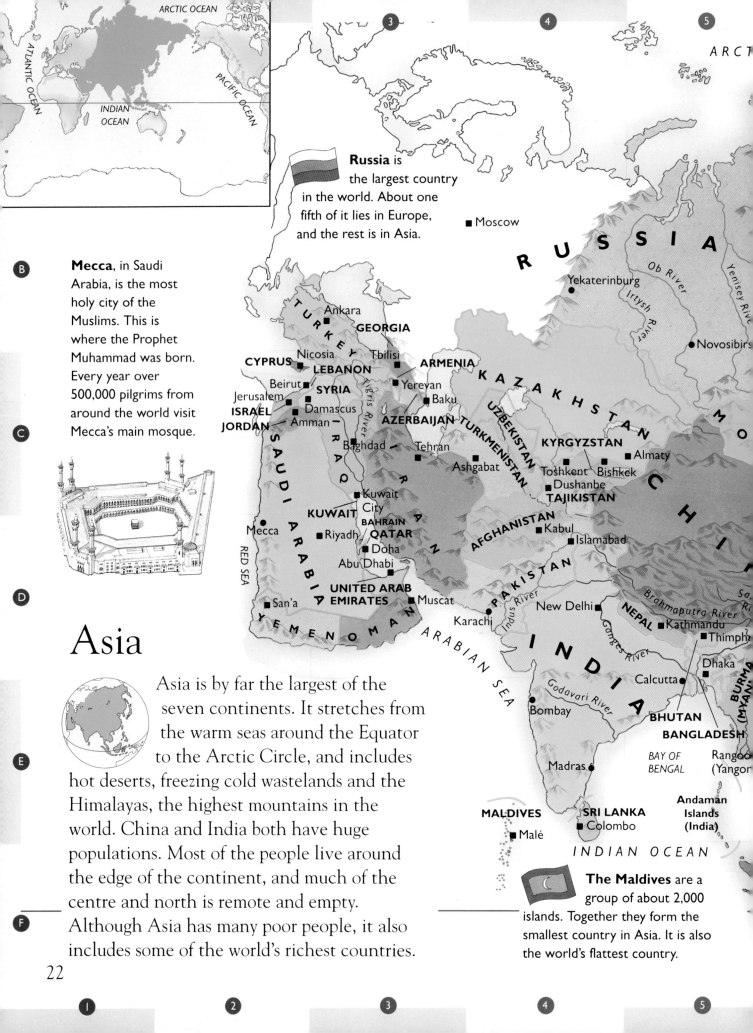

ARCTIC OCEAN

ATLANTIC OCEAN

INDIAN OCEAN

PACIFIC OCEAN

**Russia** is the largest country in the world. About one fifth of it lies in Europe, and the rest is in Asia.

**Mecca**, in Saudi Arabia, is the most holy city of the Muslims. This is where the Prophet Muhammad was born. Every year over 500,000 pilgrims from around the world visit Mecca's main mosque.

# Asia

Asia is by far the largest of the seven continents. It stretches from the warm seas around the Equator to the Arctic Circle, and includes hot deserts, freezing cold wastelands and the Himalayas, the highest mountains in the world. China and India both have huge populations. Most of the people live around the edge of the continent, and much of the centre and north is remote and empty. Although Asia has many poor people, it also includes some of the world's richest countries.

**The Maldives** are a group of about 2,000 islands. Together they form the smallest country in Asia. It is also the world's flattest country.

ARCTIC

■ Moscow

R U S S I A

Ob River
Yekaterinburg
Irtysh River
Yenisey River
● Novosibirs

T U R K E Y
Ankara
**GEORGIA**
Tbilisi
**ARMENIA**
**CYPRUS**
Nicosia
**LEBANON**
Beirut
Yerevan
**SYRIA**
Jerusalem
Damascus
**AZERBAIJAN**
Baku
**ISRAEL**
Amman
**JORDAN**
Baghdad
I R A Q
Tehran
**TURKMENISTAN**
Ashgabat
**UZBEKISTAN**
Toshkent
**KAZAKHSTAN**
**KYRGYZSTAN**
Almaty
Bishkek
Dushanbe
**TAJIKISTAN**
C H I
M O
I R A N

S A U D I   A R A B I A
Kuwait City
**KUWAIT**
**BAHRAIN**
**QATAR**
Mecca
Riyadh
Doha
Abu Dhabi
**AFGHANISTAN**
Kabul
Islamabad
**UNITED ARAB EMIRATES**
San'a
Muscat
P A K I S T A N
Indus River
New Delhi
**NEPAL**
Kathmandu
Brahmaputra River
**BHUTAN**
Thimph
Y E M E N   O M A N
RED SEA
ARABIAN SEA
Karachi
I N D I A
Ganges River
Dhaka
Calcutta
**BANGLADESH**
BURMA (MYANM
Godavari River
Bombay
BAY OF BENGAL
Rangoo (Yangor
Madras
**MALDIVES**
Malé
**SRI LANKA**
Colombo
Andaman Islands (India)
I N D I A N   O C E A N

22

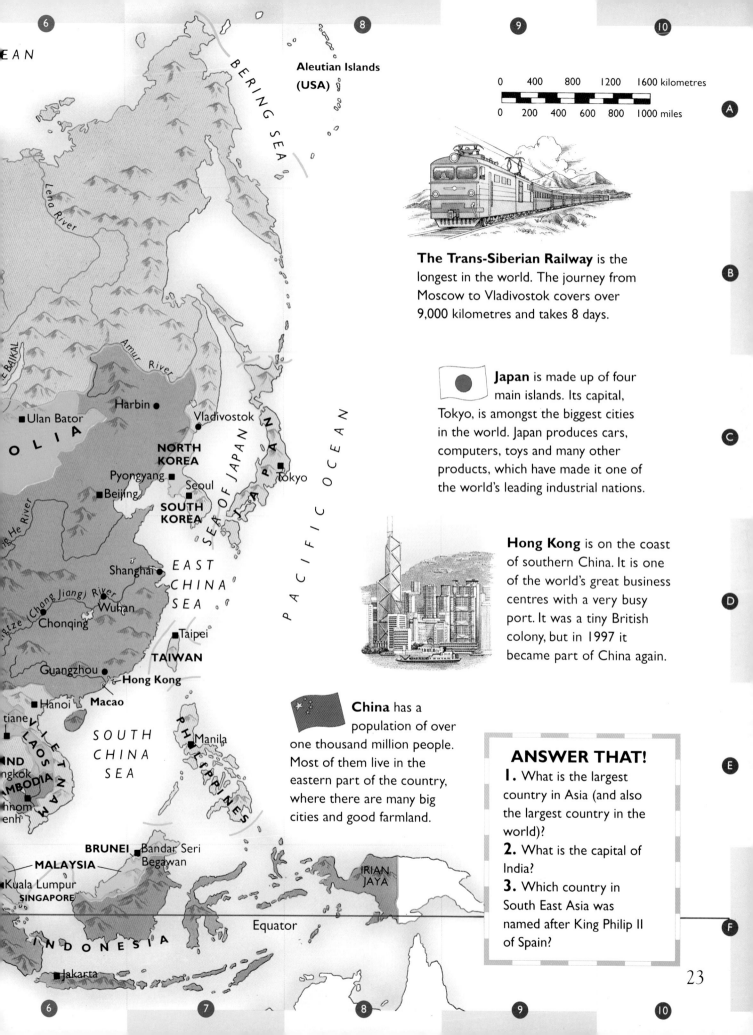

Aleutian Islands
(USA)

BERING SEA

Lena River

Amur River

LAKE BAIKAL

■ Ulan Bator

OLIA

Harbin ●

Vladivostok

NORTH
KOREA

Pyongyang ■

Beijing ■

Seoul ■

SOUTH
KOREA

■ Tokyo

SEA OF JAPAN

JAPAN

PACIFIC OCEAN

Huang He River

Shanghai ●

EAST
CHINA
SEA

Yangtze (Chang Jiang) River

Wuhan ●

Chonqing ●

■ Taipei

TAIWAN

Guangzhou ●

◆ Hong Kong

Macao

■ Hanoi

tiane ■

LAOS

VIETNAM

SOUTH
CHINA
SEA

PHILIPPINES

● Manila

ND

ngkok

MBODIA ■

hnom
enh ■

BRUNEI ■ Bandar Seri
Begawan

MALAYSIA

■ Kuala Lumpur

SINGAPORE

IRIAN
JAYA

Equator

INDONESIA

■ Jakarta

**Scale:**
0   400   800   1200   1600 kilometres
0   200   400   600   800   1000 miles

**The Trans-Siberian Railway** is the longest in the world. The journey from Moscow to Vladivostok covers over 9,000 kilometres and takes 8 days.

**Japan** is made up of four main islands. Its capital, Tokyo, is amongst the biggest cities in the world. Japan produces cars, computers, toys and many other products, which have made it one of the world's leading industrial nations.

**Hong Kong** is on the coast of southern China. It is one of the world's great business centres with a very busy port. It was a tiny British colony, but in 1997 it became part of China again.

**China** has a population of over one thousand million people. Most of them live in the eastern part of the country, where there are many big cities and good farmland.

## ANSWER THAT!

**1.** What is the largest country in Asia (and also the largest country in the world)?

**2.** What is the capital of India?

**3.** Which country in South East Asia was named after King Philip II of Spain?

A B C D E F

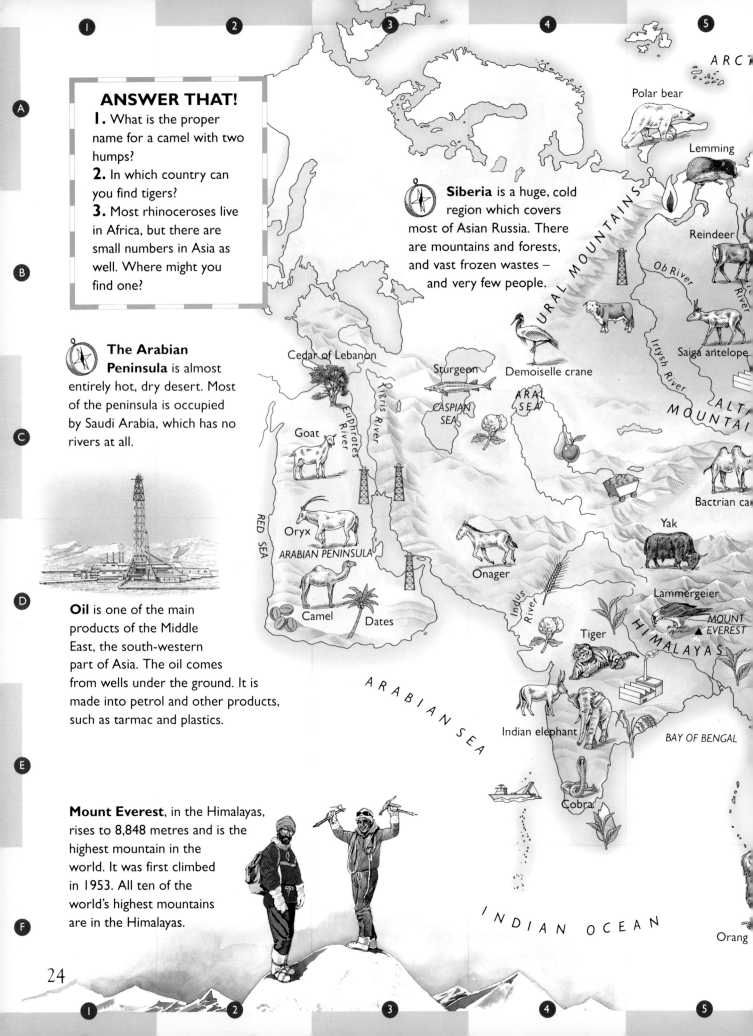

## ANSWER THAT!

**1.** What is the proper name for a camel with two humps?

**2.** In which country can you find tigers?

**3.** Most rhinoceroses live in Africa, but there are small numbers in Asia as well. Where might you find one?

### The Arabian Peninsula is almost entirely hot, dry desert. Most of the peninsula is occupied by Saudi Arabia, which has no rivers at all.

**Oil** is one of the main products of the Middle East, the south-western part of Asia. The oil comes from wells under the ground. It is made into petrol and other products, such as tarmac and plastics.

**Mount Everest**, in the Himalayas, rises to **8,848** metres and is the highest mountain in the world. It was first climbed in 1953. All ten of the world's highest mountains are in the Himalayas.

**Siberia** is a huge, cold region which covers most of Asian Russia. There are mountains and forests, and vast frozen wastes – and very few people.

ARCTI

Polar bear

Lemming

Reindeer

URAL MOUNTAINS

Ob River

Irtysh River

River

Saiga antelope

Cedar of Lebanon

Sturgeon

Demoiselle crane

ARAL SEA

ALTA
MOUNTAI

CASPIAN SEA

Euphrates River

Tigris River

Goat

Bactrian ca

Yak

Oryx

ARABIAN PENINSULA

Onager

Lammergeier

MOUNT EVEREST

RED SEA

Indus River

HIMALAYAS

Tiger

Camel

Dates

ARABIAN SEA

Indian elephant

BAY OF BENGAL

Cobra

INDIAN OCEAN

Orang

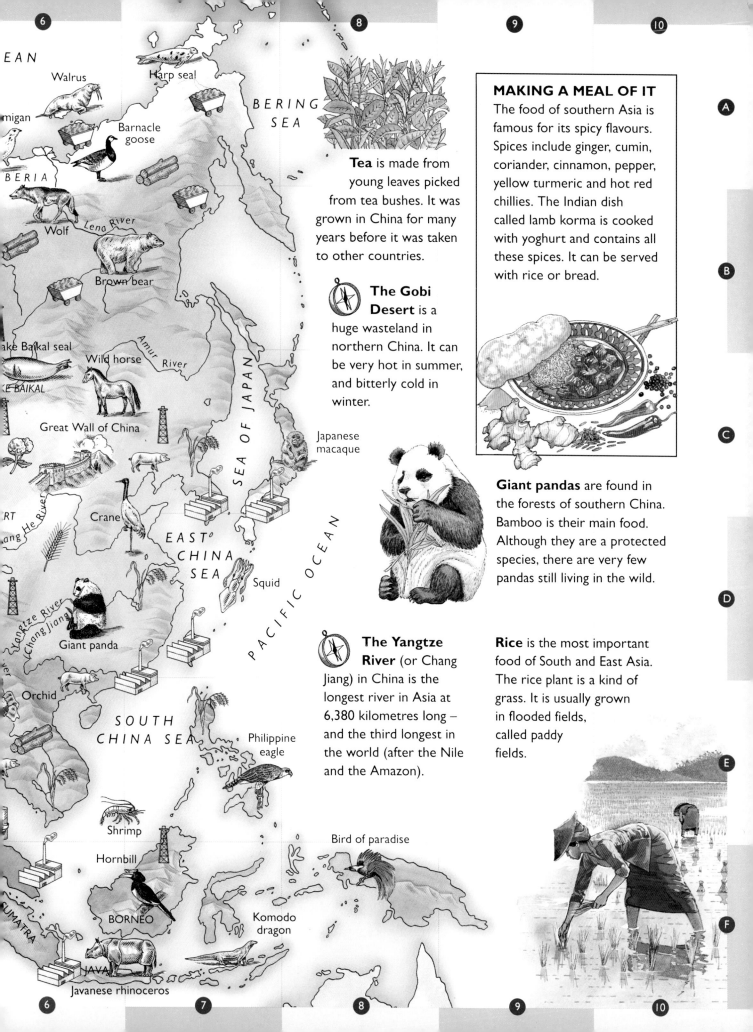

EAN

Walrus

migan

Harp seal

BERING
SEA

Barnacle
goose

BERIA

Wolf

Lena River

Brown bear

ake Baikal seal

KE BAIKAL

Amur River

Wild horse

Great Wall of China

SEA OF JAPAN

Japanese
macaque

RT

ang He River

Crane

EAST
CHINA
SEA

Squid

PACIFIC OCEAN

Yangtze River

Chang Jiang

Giant panda

Orchid

SOUTH
CHINA SEA

Philippine
eagle

Shrimp

Hornbill

Bird of paradise

BORNEO

Komodo
dragon

SUMATRA

JAVA

Javanese rhinoceros

**Tea** is made from young leaves picked from tea bushes. It was grown in China for many years before it was taken to other countries.

**The Gobi Desert** is a huge wasteland in northern China. It can be very hot in summer, and bitterly cold in winter.

## MAKING A MEAL OF IT

The food of southern Asia is famous for its spicy flavours. Spices include ginger, cumin, coriander, cinnamon, pepper, yellow turmeric and hot red chillies. The Indian dish called lamb korma is cooked with yoghurt and contains all these spices. It can be served with rice or bread.

**Giant pandas** are found in the forests of southern China. Bamboo is their main food. Although they are a protected species, there are very few pandas still living in the wild.

**The Yangtze River** (or Chang Jiang) in China is the longest river in Asia at 6,380 kilometres long – and the third longest in the world (after the Nile and the Amazon).

**Rice** is the most important food of South and East Asia. The rice plant is a kind of grass. It is usually grown in flooded fields, called paddy fields.

A
B
C
D
E
F

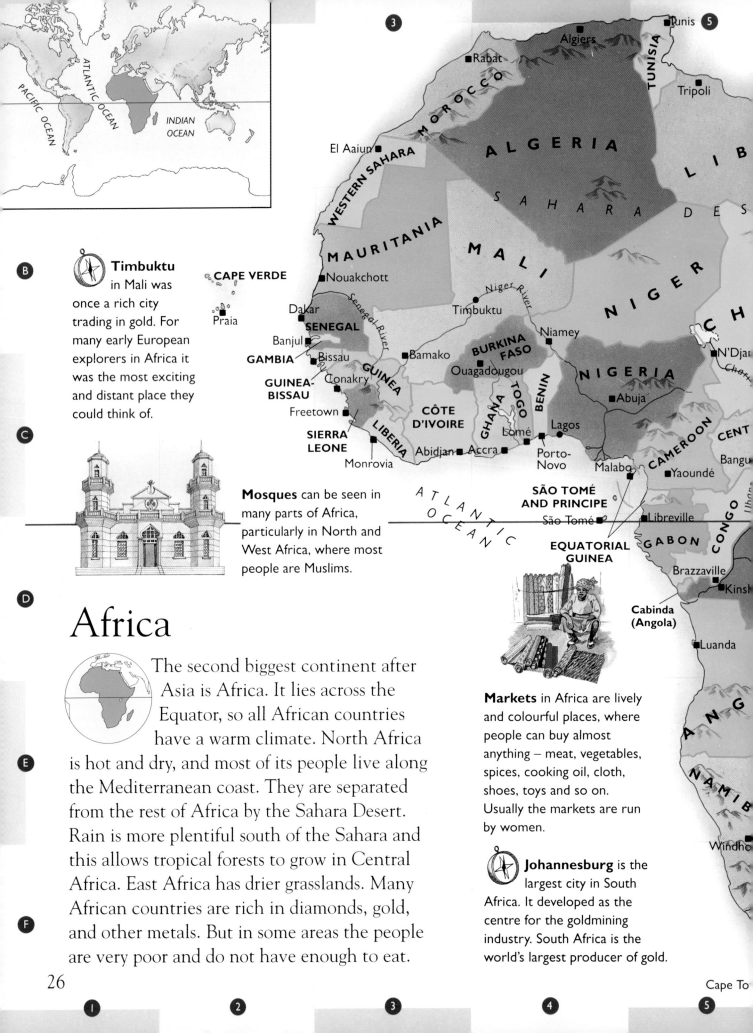

**Timbuktu** in Mali was once a rich city trading in gold. For many early European explorers in Africa it was the most exciting and distant place they could think of.

**Mosques** can be seen in many parts of Africa, particularly in North and West Africa, where most people are Muslims.

# Africa

The second biggest continent after Asia is Africa. It lies across the Equator, so all African countries have a warm climate. North Africa is hot and dry, and most of its people live along the Mediterranean coast. They are separated from the rest of Africa by the Sahara Desert. Rain is more plentiful south of the Sahara and this allows tropical forests to grow in Central Africa. East Africa has drier grasslands. Many African countries are rich in diamonds, gold, and other metals. But in some areas the people are very poor and do not have enough to eat.

**Markets** in Africa are lively and colourful places, where people can buy almost anything – meat, vegetables, spices, cooking oil, cloth, shoes, toys and so on. Usually the markets are run by women.

**Johannesburg** is the largest city in South Africa. It developed as the centre for the goldmining industry. South Africa is the world's largest producer of gold.

ATLANTIC OCEAN

PACIFIC OCEAN

INDIAN OCEAN

**CAPE VERDE**

WESTERN SAHARA

MOROCCO

Rabat

Algiers

TUNISIA

Tripoli

ALGERIA

SAHARA

LIB

DES

El Aaiun

MAURITANIA

MALI

NIGER

CH

Nouakchott

Dakar

**SENEGAL**

Banjul

**GAMBIA**

Bissau

**GUINEA-BISSAU**

Conakry

GUINEA

Freetown

**SIERRA LEONE**

LIBERIA

Monrovia

Praia

Senegal River

Niger River

Timbuktu

Niamey

Bamako

**BURKINA FASO**

Ouagadougou

CÔTE D'IVOIRE

GHANA

TOGO

BENIN

Lomé

Abidjan

Accra

Porto-Novo

NIGERIA

Abuja

Lagos

N'Djar

Chai

CAMEROON

Yaoundé

CENT

Bangu

Malabo

**SÃO TOMÉ AND PRINCIPE**

São Tomé

**EQUATORIAL GUINEA**

GABON

CONGO

Libreville

Brazzaville

Kinsh

**Cabinda (Angola)**

Luanda

ANG

NAMIB

Windho

A T L A N T I C   O C E A N

MEDITERRANEAN
SEA

Alexandria ■ Cairo

EGYPT

Nile River

RED SEA

SUDAN

Khartoum ■

Asmera ■

ERITREA

Blue Nile River

White Nile River

DJIBOUTI
■ Djibouti

ETHIOPIA

Addis Ababa ■

Shabelle River

SOMALIA

ICAN
UBLIC

UGANDA

KENYA

Mogadishu ■

Kampala ■

re River

RWANDA
■ Kigali

■ Nairobi

INDIAN OCEAN

Equator

BURUNDI
■ Bujumbura

CRATIC
IC OF
NGO

SEYCHELLES
Victoria ■

Dodoma ■

TANZANIA

Dar es Salaam ■

A

MALAWI

COMOROS
■ Moroni

ZAMBIA

■ Lilongwe

■ Mayotte
(France)

Lusaka ■

Zambezi River

MOZAMBIQUE

MADAGASCAR

Harare ■

ZIMBABWE

TSWANA

Limpopo River

Antananarivo ■

MAURITIUS

orone ■

Pretoria ■

Maputo ■

Réunion
(France)

Port Louis

Johannesburg ■

SWAZILAND
■ Mbabane

LESOTHO
■ Maseru

ge

OUTH
RICA

**Cairo** is the capital of Egypt. It has a population of over 7 million, making it easily the largest city in Africa. The Nile River flows through the city.

**The pyramids** lie just outside Cairo. They were built as giant tombs for the Egyptian kings over four thousand years ago. They are guarded by a stone Sphinx – half man, half cat.

**Sudan** is the largest country in Africa. The White Nile flows through the length of the country. The capital, Khartoum, lies at the place where the White Nile and the Blue Nile meet to become the Nile River.

**The Seychelles** is a group of about 100 islands off the east coast of Africa. This is the smallest country in the region. The islands are famous for their beautiful white-sand beaches.

### ANSWER THAT!
**1.** Since 1992 Nigeria has had a new capital. What is the capital called?
**2.** Two countries in Africa begin with the letter Z. Can you name both of them?
**3.** What is the name of the country that lies inside the borders of Senegal?

kilometres
0    400    800    1200    1600

0    200    400    600    800    1000
miles

## MAKING A MEAL OF IT

African cookery varies from region to region. In North Africa, the most famous dish is couscous – fluffy grains of steamed wheat. In West Africa, meat stews are often cooked with a peanut sauce spiced with dried shrimps. (Peanuts are also called groundnuts.) The stews are eaten with sliced root vegetables, such as yams.

**The Sahara Desert** is the largest desert in the world. Much of it is covered by huge sand dunes, but some parts have high, rocky mountains. Camels are used to carry goods and people in desert areas.

### ANSWER THAT!

**1.** What is the name of the lizard from Madagascar that can change colour to match its background?
**2.** If you wanted to cross the Sahara Desert, what animal would you take to carry your baggage?
**3.** Which animal's name begins with two A's?

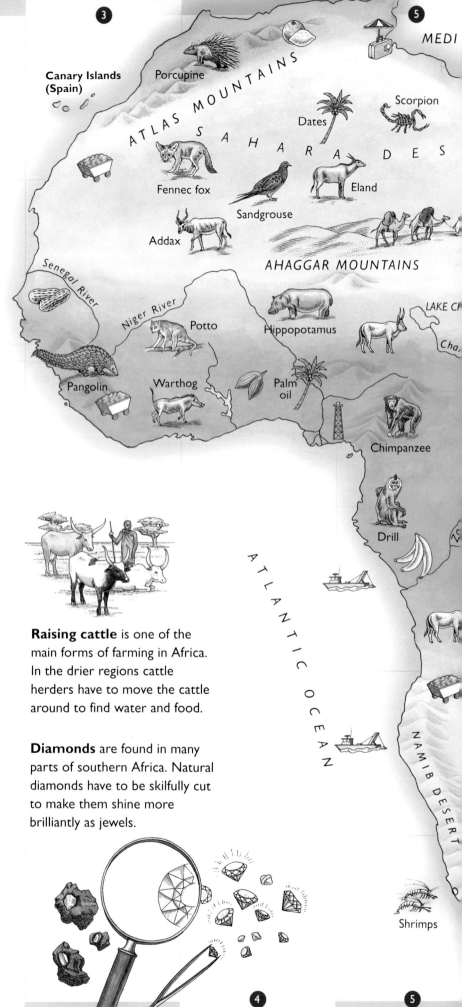

MEDI

Canary Islands (Spain)

Porcupine

ATLAS MOUNTAINS

SAHARA DES

Dates

Scorpion

Fennec fox

Sandgrouse

Eland

Addax

AHAGGAR MOUNTAINS

Senegal River

LAKE CH

Niger River

Potto

Hippopotamus

Cha

Pangolin

Warthog

Palm oil

Chimpanzee

Drill

ATLANTIC OCEAN

**Raising cattle** is one of the main forms of farming in Africa. In the drier regions cattle herders have to move the cattle around to find water and food.

**Diamonds** are found in many parts of southern Africa. Natural diamonds have to be skilfully cut to make them shine more brilliantly as jewels.

NAMIB DESERT

Shrimps

AN SEA

Camel

Oryx

**Coffee** is made from the seeds of the coffee plant. It was probably first grown in Ethiopia.

RED SEA

Nile River

**The River Nile** is the longest river in the world. It flows 6,670 kilometres, from its source at Lake Victoria to the Mediterranean Sea.

Leopard

Blue Nile River

Hornbill

White Nile River

Acacia tree

Nubian goat

Shabelle River

Aardvark

Cheetah

Lion

**The African elephant** is the world's largest living animal on land. Elephants can grow to over 3 metres tall and weigh 6 tonnes. Some elephants live to over 70 years of age.

LAKE VICTORIA

**Lake Victoria** is the largest lake in Africa, and the third largest lake in the world. It lies between three countries: Kenya, Tanzania and Uganda.

LAKE TANGANYIKA

MOUNT KILIMANJARO

Giraffe

**Mount Kilimanjaro** in Tanzania is the highest mountain in Africa. Its tallest peak rises to 5,895 metres, and is covered with snow throughout the year.

Zebra

LAKE MALAWI

Hyena

Gemsbok

MADAGASCAR

Zambezi River

Chameleon

Hartebeest

Ring-tailed lemur

INDIAN OCEAN

HARI RT

Limpopo River

**Madagascar** is the largest island off Africa. Some of its wildlife is found only in Madagascar – such as the ring-tailed lemur, a relative of the monkey family.

Wildebeest

Whale

Cape baboon

kats

ch

la

A

B

C

D

E

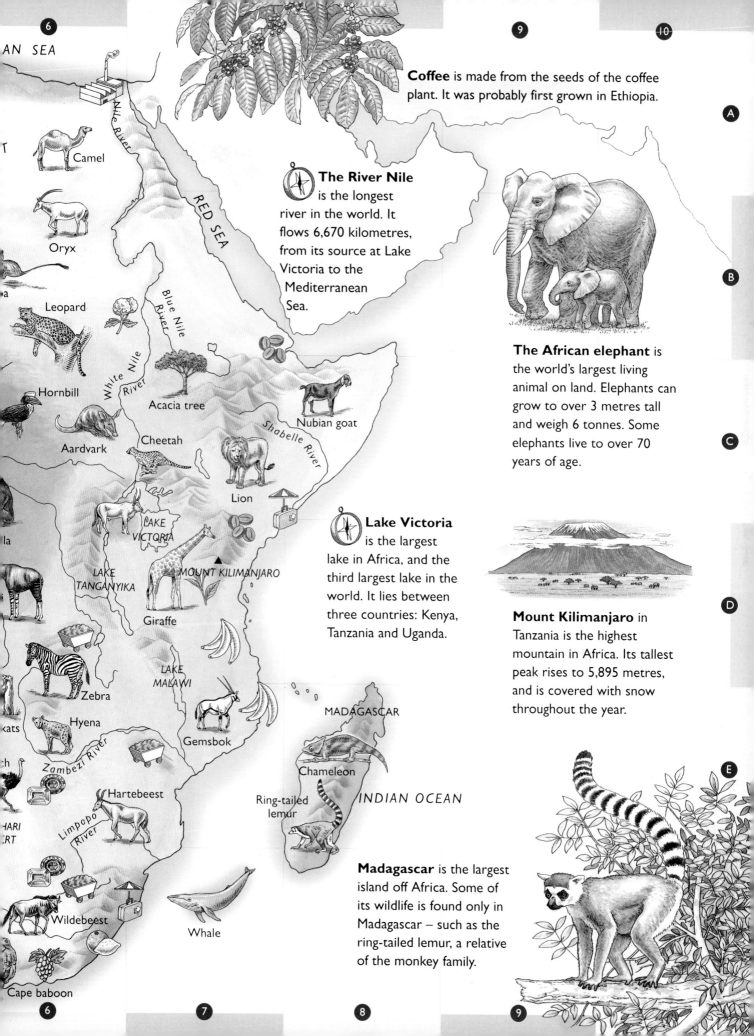

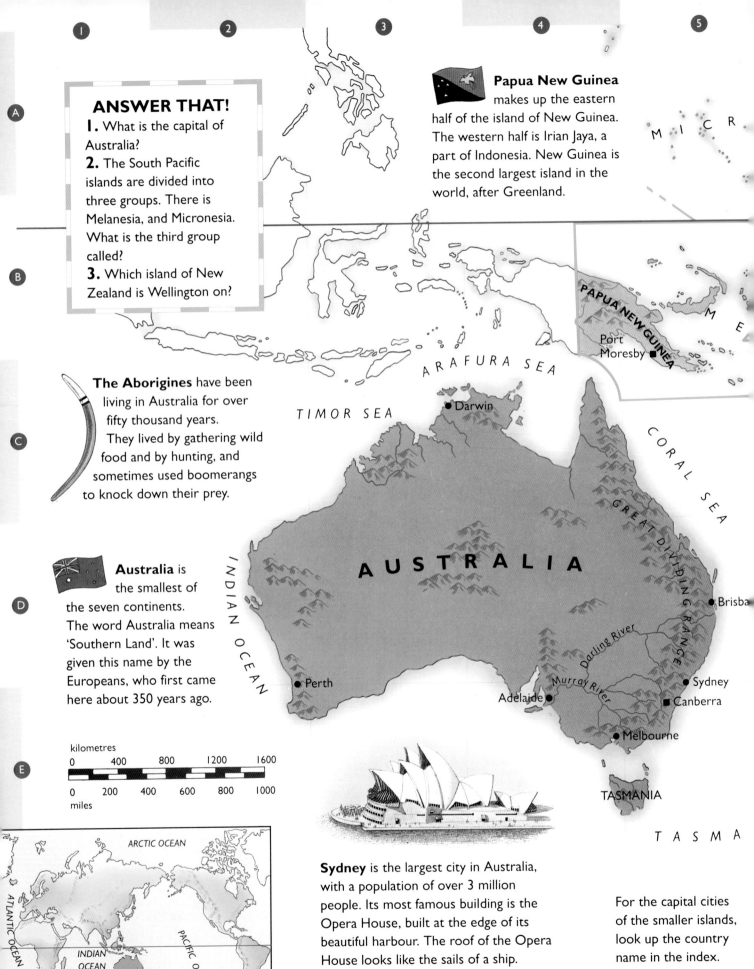

**ANSWER THAT!**
**1.** What is the capital of Australia?
**2.** The South Pacific islands are divided into three groups. There is Melanesia, and Micronesia. What is the third group called?
**3.** Which island of New Zealand is Wellington on?

**Papua New Guinea** makes up the eastern half of the island of New Guinea. The western half is Irian Jaya, a part of Indonesia. New Guinea is the second largest island in the world, after Greenland.

M I C R

PAPUA NEW GUINEA

M E

Port Moresby ■

**The Aborigines** have been living in Australia for over fifty thousand years. They lived by gathering wild food and by hunting, and sometimes used boomerangs to knock down their prey.

ARAFURA SEA

TIMOR SEA

• Darwin

CORAL SEA

GREAT DIVIDING RANGE

**Australia** is the smallest of the seven continents. The word Australia means 'Southern Land'. It was given this name by the Europeans, who first came here about 350 years ago.

A U S T R A L I A

INDIAN OCEAN

• Perth

Darling River

Murray River

• Brisba

• Sydney

Adelaide ●

■ Canberra

• Melbourne

kilometres
| 0 | 400 | 800 | 1200 | 1600 |

| 0 | 200 | 400 | 600 | 800 | 1000 |
miles

TASMANIA

T A S M A

ARCTIC OCEAN

ATLANTIC OCEAN

INDIAN OCEAN

PACIFIC OCEAN

**Sydney** is the largest city in Australia, with a population of over 3 million people. Its most famous building is the Opera House, built at the edge of its beautiful harbour. The roof of the Opera House looks like the sails of a ship.

For the capital cities of the smaller islands, look up the country name in the index.

**Nauru** is a tiny island which is just 21 square kilometres in size. This makes it one of the smallest independent countries in the world.

**The Polynesian islands** lie in the middle of the South Pacific Ocean. Islanders used to travel vast distances between the islands in small sailing boats.

PACIFIC OCEAN

Equator

RSHALL ISLANDS

E S I A

ERATED TES OF RONESIA

**NAURU**

**KIRIBATI**

OLOMON ISLANDS

Honiara

P O L Y N E S I A

**TUVALU**

**Tokelau (NZ)**

N E S I A

**VANUATU**

Vila

**Wallis and Futuna (France)**

**SAMOA**

Apia

**American Samoa (USA)**

Suva

**TONGA**

**FIJI**

Nuku'alofa

**Niue (NZ)**

**Cook Islands (NZ)**

**French Polynesia (France)**

Caledonia (France)

**New Zealand** lies some 2,500 kilometres om Australia. It is made up of o main islands. Most people e on the North Island, where uckland is the largest city.

**Kermadec Islands (NZ)**

North Island

Auckland

EA

South land

N E W Z E A L A N D

Wellington

Christchurch

**Chatham Island (NZ)**

# Australia and the Pacific Islands

Australia is so big that it is called a continent. It is about the same size as the USA, without Alaska. The cities are all close to the coast. Inland, there are vast farms where sheep and cattle are raised, but most of the middle of Australia is hot desert.

Like Australia, New Zealand is mainly English-speaking. Here the weather is mild, and snow falls on the mountains in winter. To the north is the Pacific Ocean, with thousands of warm, tropical islands. They include tiny islands, such as Nauru, which are among the smallest nations in the world.

31

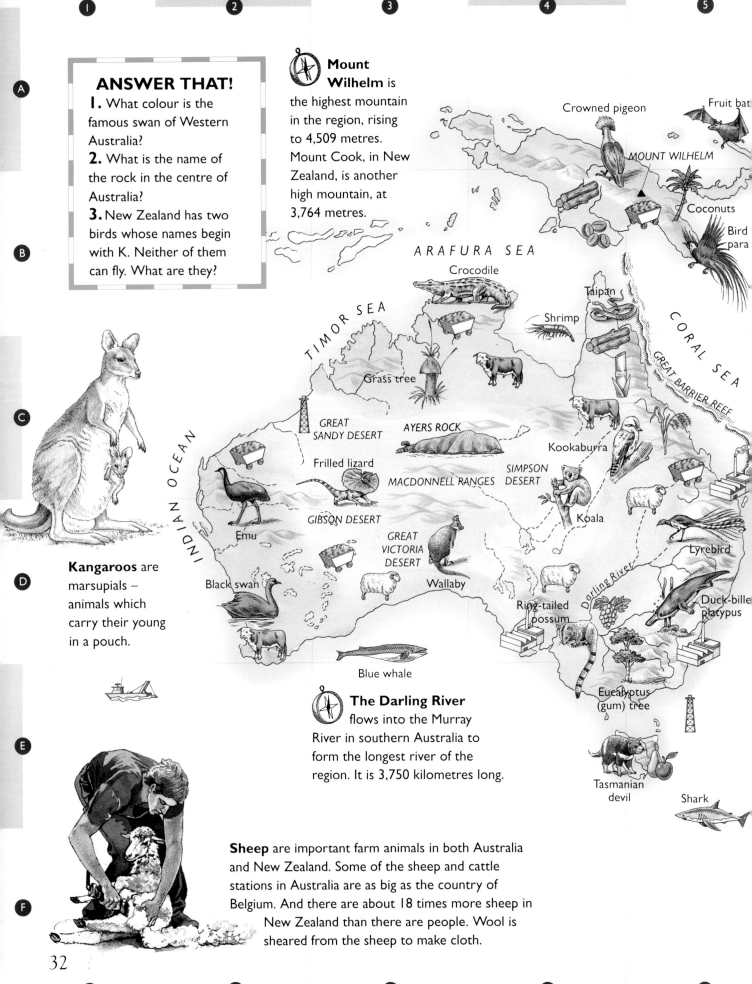

## ANSWER THAT!

**1.** What colour is the famous swan of Western Australia?

**2.** What is the name of the rock in the centre of Australia?

**3.** New Zealand has two birds whose names begin with K. Neither of them can fly. What are they?

**Mount Wilhelm** is the highest mountain in the region, rising to 4,509 metres. Mount Cook, in New Zealand, is another high mountain, at 3,764 metres.

MOUNT WILHELM

Crowned pigeon

Fruit bat

Coconuts

Bird para

ARAFURA SEA

Crocodile

Taipan

Shrimp

CORAL SEA

GREAT BARRIER REEF

TIMOR SEA

Grass tree

INDIAN OCEAN

GREAT SANDY DESERT

AYERS ROCK

Frilled lizard

MACDONNELL RANGES

SIMPSON DESERT

Kookaburra

Koala

GIBSON DESERT

Emu

GREAT VICTORIA DESERT

Lyrebird

Black swan

Wallaby

Ring-tailed possum

Darling River

Duck-billed platypus

**Kangaroos** are marsupials – animals which carry their young in a pouch.

Blue whale

Eucalyptus (gum) tree

**The Darling River** flows into the Murray River in southern Australia to form the longest river of the region. It is 3,750 kilometres long.

Tasmanian devil

Shark

**Sheep** are important farm animals in both Australia and New Zealand. Some of the sheep and cattle stations in Australia are as big as the country of Belgium. And there are about 18 times more sheep in New Zealand than there are people. Wool is sheared from the sheep to make cloth.

Anemone fish

Coconuts　　Sweet lips

Giant clam

**The Great Barrier Reef** is the longest coral reef in the world. It stretches about 2,000 kilometres. The hard coral is made by tiny sea animals called polyps.

utterfly fish　　Coconuts

Auger shell

Kagu

Tonna shell

Fairy tern

Wandering albatross

Wrasse

**Coconut palms** are grown on many of the South Pacific islands.

P A C I F I C   O C E A N

Tuna

**Geysers** gush up from the ground at Rotorua, New Zealand. They are like fountains of hot water. The water is heated by volcanic activity under the ground.

**MAKING A MEAL OF IT**
The warm weather of Australia is ideal for eating outdoors, and Australians love to have barbecues. They cook large steaks, as well as lamb, fish and prawns. For dessert they can have home-grown fruit, such as bananas, kiwi-fruit, pineapple, peaches and watermelon.

Tuatara

ASMAN SEA

●Rotorua

Kakapo

Takahe

Shrimp

MOUNT COOK

Kiwi

33

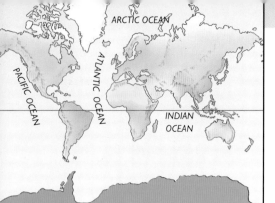

The extent of the Arctic and Antarctic ice varies from summer to winter. This ice is known as pack ice.

**Icebergs** are huge blocks of ice which float in the seas close to Antarctica and the Arctic. Most of an iceberg is hidden beneath the water. Icebergs can be very dangerous to ships.

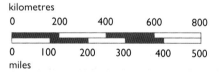

kilometres

| 0 | 200 | 400 | 600 | 800 |

| 0 | 100 | 200 | 300 | 400 | 500 |

miles

**ANSWER THAT!**

**1.** Which two kinds of seal are named after animals living in Africa?
**2.** Which stinging insect lives around the Arctic?
**3.** One kind of bird can be seen in both Antarctica and the Arctic because it flies from one to the other. What is its name?

**The lowest temperature** ever recorded comes from the Vostok research station: 89° Centigrade below freezing. Antarctica is colder than the Arctic because the land takes longer to warm up in the summer sunlight.

**The Vinson Massif** is the highest mountain in Antarctica rising to 5,140 metres. Mount Erebus is the highest active volcano.

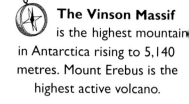

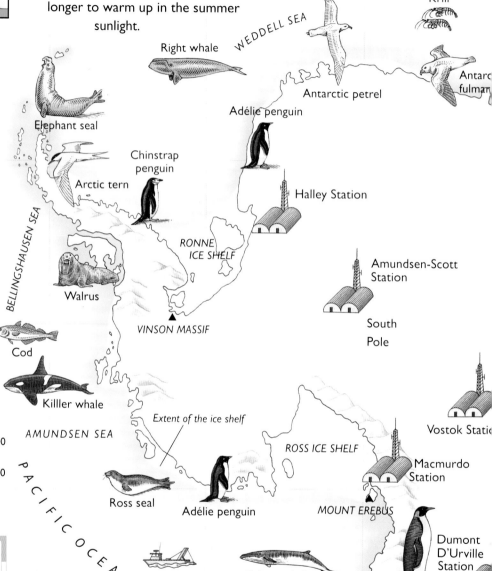

Krill

Right whale

WEDDELL SEA

Antarctic petrel

Antarctic fulmar

Adélie penguin

Elephant seal

Halley Station

Chinstrap penguin

Arctic tern

Amundsen-Scott Station

BELLINGSHAUSEN SEA

RONNE ICE SHELF

Walrus

South Pole

Cod

VINSON MASSIF

Killer whale

Vostok Station

Extent of the ice shelf

AMUNDSEN SEA

ROSS ICE SHELF

Macmurdo Station

PACIFIC OCEAN

Ross seal

Adélie penguin

MOUNT EREBUS

Dumont D'Urville Station

Baleen whale

Emperor penguin

**Penguins** are found only in the southern parts of the world, particularly around the edges of Antarctica. Emperor penguins are the largest kind. The males look after the eggs through the cold Antarctic winter and raise the young when they hatch.

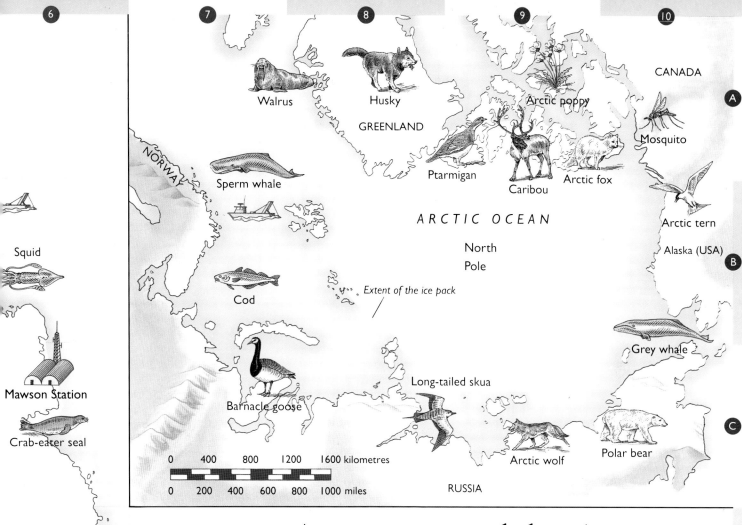

CANADA

Walrus
Husky
Arctic poppy
GREENLAND
Mosquito
Ptarmigan
Caribou
Arctic fox
Sperm whale
NORWAY
Arctic tern
ARCTIC OCEAN
Alaska (USA)
North
Pole
Cod
Extent of the ice pack
Grey whale
Squid
Barnacle goose
Long-tailed skua
Mawson Station
Crab-eater seal
Arctic wolf
Polar bear

0   400   800   1200   1600 kilometres

0   200   400   600   800   1000 miles

RUSSIA

South Polar
skua

INDIAN OCEAN

Casey Base

opard seal

**Scientific stations** carry
out research in various parts
of Antarctica, usually during
the short summer. The
scientists study such things
as weather patterns and
animal life.

# Antarctica and the Arctic

The very top and bottom of the world
are the places which receive the least
sunlight, and in winter they get no
sunlight at all. These regions are bitterly
cold, and covered with thick layers of ice and
snow. The furthest point south on our world is
called the South Pole, and the furthest point north
is called the North Pole.

The South Pole is actually on land, in the middle
of the continent called Antarctica. The North
Pole is not on land at all, but on a huge sheet of ice
in the middle of the Arctic Ocean. The size of the
ice sheet changes as the ice melts and freezes
during the year. The Inuit live around the
edge of the Arctic. The only people in
Antarctica are explorers and scientists.

A
B
C
D
E
F

35

# Flags of the World

## North America

CANADA

UNITED STATES OF AMERICA

MEXICO

GUATEMALA

BELIZE

EL SALVADOR

HONDURAS

NICARAGUA

COSTA RICA

PANAMA

BAHAMAS

CUBA

JAMAICA

HAITI

DOMINICAN REPUBLIC

ANTIGUA AND BARBUDA

ST KITTS AND NEVIS

DOMINICA

ST LUCIA

BARBADOS

GRENADA

ST VINCENT AND THE GRENADINES

TRINIDAD AND TOBAGO

## South America

VENEZUELA

GUYANA

SURINAM

BRAZIL

COLOMBIA

ECUADOR

PERU

BOLIVIA

## Europe

PARAGUAY

URUGUAY

CHILE

ARGENTINA

ICELAND

NORWAY

SWEDEN

FINLAND

DENMARK

IRELAND

UNITED KINGDOM

NETHERLANDS

BELGIUM

LUXEMBOURG

FRANCE

MONACO

SPAIN

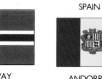
ANDORRA

PORTUGAL

ITALY

SAN MARINO

VATICAN CITY STATE

MALTA

SWITZERLAND

LIECHTENSTEIN

AUSTRIA

GERMANY

POLAND

CZECH REPUBLIC

SLOVAKIA

HUNGARY

SLOVENIA

CROATIA

BOSNIA-HERZEGOVINA

YUGOSLAVIA

MACEDONIA

ALBANIA

GREECE

BULGARIA

ROMANIA

RUSSIA

ESTONIA

LATVIA

LITHUANIA

BELARUS

UKRAINE

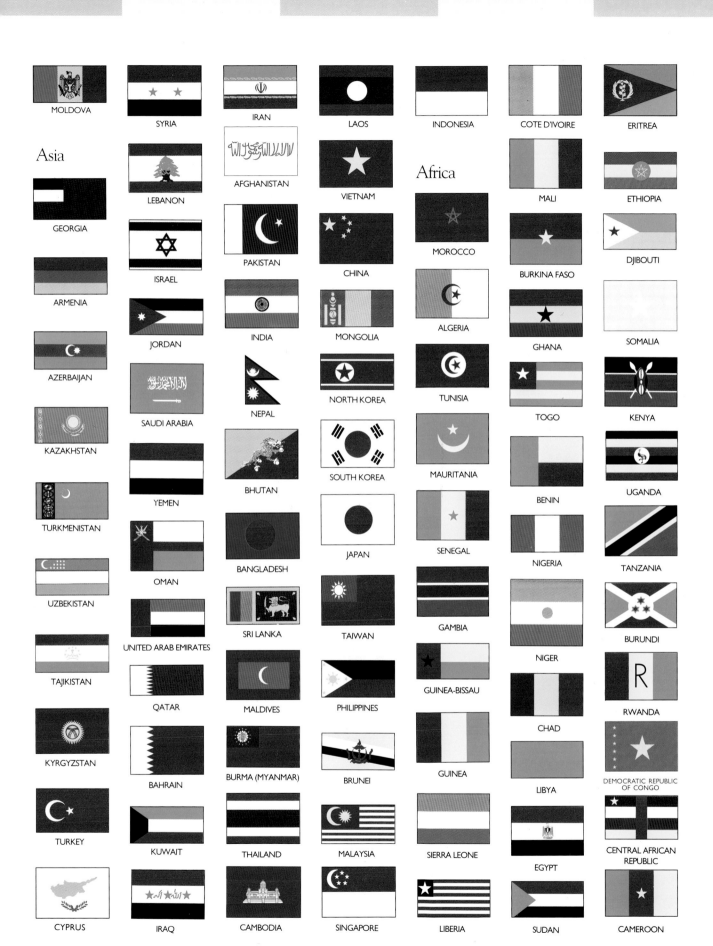

MOLDOVA

Asia

GEORGIA

ARMENIA

AZERBAIJAN

KAZAKHSTAN

TURKMENISTAN

UZBEKISTAN

TAJIKISTAN

KYRGYZSTAN

TURKEY

CYPRUS

SYRIA

LEBANON

ISRAEL

JORDAN

SAUDI ARABIA

YEMEN

OMAN

UNITED ARAB EMIRATES

QATAR

BAHRAIN

KUWAIT

IRAQ

IRAN

AFGHANISTAN

PAKISTAN

INDIA

NEPAL

BHUTAN

BANGLADESH

SRI LANKA

MALDIVES

BURMA (MYANMAR)

THAILAND

CAMBODIA

LAOS

VIETNAM

CHINA

MONGOLIA

NORTH KOREA

SOUTH KOREA

JAPAN

TAIWAN

PHILIPPINES

BRUNEI

MALAYSIA

SINGAPORE

INDONESIA

Africa

MOROCCO

ALGERIA

TUNISIA

MAURITANIA

SENEGAL

GAMBIA

GUINEA-BISSAU

GUINEA

SIERRA LEONE

LIBERIA

COTE D'IVOIRE

MALI

BURKINA FASO

GHANA

TOGO

BENIN

NIGERIA

NIGER

CHAD

LIBYA

EGYPT

SUDAN

ERITREA

ETHIOPIA

DJIBOUTI

SOMALIA

KENYA

UGANDA

TANZANIA

BURUNDI

RWANDA

DEMOCRATIC REPUBLIC
OF CONGO

CENTRAL AFRICAN
REPUBLIC

CAMEROON

37

EQUATORIAL GUINEA

LESOTHO

MARSHALL ISLANDS

GABON

SWAZILAND

SOLOMON ISLANDS

SAO TOME AND PRINCIPE

MADAGASCAR

NAURU

CONGO

CAPE VERDE

TUVALU

ANGOLA

SEYCHELLES

KIRIBATI

ZAMBIA

COMOROS

VANUATU

MALAWI

MAURITIUS

FIJI

MOZAMBIQUE

Australia and the Pacific

TONGA

ZIMBABWE

PAPUA NEW GUINEA

SAMOA

BOTSWANA

AUSTRALIA

NAMIBIA

NEW ZEALAND

SOUTH AFRICA

FEDERATED STATES OF MICRONESIA

## ANSWER THAT!

*page 11*
1. Mexico
2. Cuba
3. Greenland

*page 13*
1. Narwhal
2. Maize (sweet corn)
3. Rattlesnake

*page 15*
1. Two, Brazil and Bolivia
2. Chile
3. Colombia

*page 16*
1. Sloth
2. Giant anteater
3. Poison arrow frog

*page 19*
1. Iceland
2. Istanbul in Turkey
3. Czech Republic

*page 21*
1. Pelican
2. Northern Russia
3. Chamois, in the Alps

*page 23*
1. Russia
2. New Delhi
3. Philippines

*page 24*
1. Bactrian camel
2. India
3. Java (Indonesia)

*page 27*
1. Abuja (it used to be Lagos)
2. Zambia and Zimbabwe
3. Gambia

*page 28*
1. Chameleon
2. Camel
3. Aardvark

*page 30*
1. Canberra
2. Polynesia
3. North Island

*page 32*
1. Black
2. Ayers Rock
3. Kiwi (the national symbol of New Zealand) and Kakapo

*page 34*
1. Leopard seal and Elephant seal
2. Mosquito
3. Arctic tern

Now you have answered all these questions, here are some other kinds of questions to ask.

*What is the capital of...?*
*Which is the largest country in...?*
*Which is the smallest country in...?*
*Where is the highest mountain in...?*
*Where is the longest river in...?*

# Index

## A

Abidjan 26 C3
Abu Dhabi 22 D3
Abuja 26 C4
Accra 26 C4
Aconcagua 17 B7
Addis Ababa 27 C7
ADELAIDE 30 E4
AFGHANISTAN 22 D4
Alaska 10 B4, 35 B10
ALBANIA 19 E6
Alexandria 27 A6
ALGERIA 26 A4
Algiers 26 A4
Almaty 22 C5
Alps 20 E4
Amazon River 14 D3,
   16 D3
American Samoa 31 C8
Amman 22 C2
Amsterdam 18 C5
Andaman Islands 22 E5
Andes Mountains
   14 A4–B5
ANDORRA 18 E5
   *capital* Andorra la Vella
Angel Falls 16 C3
ANGOLA 26 E5
Anguilla 11 F8
Ankara 22 B3
Antananarivo 27 E8
ANTIGUA AND BARBUDA
   11 F8
   *capital* St John's
Apia 31 C8
Appalachian Mountains
   13 E6–7
Arabian peninsula
   24 D2–3
Arabian Sea 22 D3–E4,
   24 E3
Aral Sea 24 C4
ARGENTINA 15 C6–8
ARMENIA 22 C3
Ashgabat 22 C4
Asmera 27 B7
Asunción 15 D6
Atacama Desert 17 B6
Athens 19 F7
Auckland 31 E7
AUSTRALIA 30, 32
AUSTRIA 19 D6
AZERBAIJAN 22 C3

## B

Baghdad 22 C3
BAHAMAS 11 E7
BAHRAIN 22 D3
   *capital* Al Manamah
Baikal, Lake 23 C6, 25 C6

Baku 22 C3
Bamako 26 B3
Bandar Seri Begawan
   23 F6
Bangkok 23 E6
BANGLADESH 22 E5
Bangui 26 C5
Banjul 26 B2
BARBADOS 11 F8
   *capital* Bridgetown
Barbuda 11 F8
Barcelona 18 E5
Bay of Biscay 18 D4
Beijing 23 C6
Beirut 22 C2
BELARUS 19 C7
BELGIUM 18 D5
Belgrade 19 E7
BELIZE 11 D8
Belmopan 11 D8
Bengal, Bay of 22 E5,
   24 E5
BENIN 26 C4
Berlin 19 D6
Bermuda 11 E7
Bern 18 D5
BHUTAN 22 E5
Bishkek 22 C4
Bissau 26 B3
Black Sea 19 E8,
   21 E7
Bogotá 14 B2
BOLIVIA 14 C5
Bombay 22 E4
Borneo 25 F6
BOSNIA-HERZEGOVINA
   19 E6
Boston 11 E6
BOTSWANA 27 E6
Brahmaputra River 22 D5
Brasília 14 E5
Bratislava 19 D6
BRAZIL 14 D4–E4
Brazzaville 26 D5
Brisbane 30 D5
BRUNEI 23 E6
Brussels 18 D5
Bucharest 19 E7
Budapest 19 D6
Buenos Aires 15 C7
Bujumbura 27 D6
BULGARIA 19 E7
BURKINA FASO 26 B4
BURMA 22 E5
BURUNDI 27 D6

## C

Cabinda 26 D5
Cairo 27 A6
Calcutta 22 E5
CAMBODIA 23 E6
CAMEROON 26 C5
CANADA  10, 12, 35 A10
Canary Islands 28 A3
Canberra 30 E5
Cape Horn 15 C9, 17 C10

Cape Town 26 F5
CAPE VERDE 26 B2
Caracas 14 C2
Caribbean Sea 11 E8,
   14 A1, 16 A2
Caspian Sea 19 D10,
   21 E9, 24 C3
Caucasus Mountains
   21 E8–9
Cayenne 14 D2
Cayman Islands 11 D8
CENTRAL AFRICAN
   REPUBLIC 27 C6
CHAD 26 B5
Chad, Lake 28 B5
Chatham Island 31 F7
Chicago 11 D6
CHILE 15 B6–8
CHINA 22 C5–6
Chisinau 19 D7
Chonqing 23 D6
Christchurch 31 F6
COLOMBIA 14 B3
Colombo 22 E4
Colorado River 11 B7,
   13 B6–7
COMOROS 27 D7
Conakry 26 C3
CONGO 26 C5–D5
Cook, Mount 33 F6
Cook Islands 31 C9
Copenhagen 19 C6
Coral Sea 30 C5,
   32 B5–C5
Corsica 18 E5
COSTA RICA 11 D9
CÔTE D'IVOIRE 26 C3
Crete 19 F7
CROATIA 19 E6
CUBA  11 D8–E8
CYPRUS  22 C2
CZECH REPUBLIC 19 D6

## D

Dakar 26 B2
Dallas 11 C7
Damascus 22 C3
Danube River 18 D5–6,
   21 E6
Dar es Salaam 27 D7
Darling River 30 D4,
   32 D4
Darwin 30 C3
DEMOCRATIC REPUBLIC OF
   CONGO 27 D6
DENMARK 19 C6
Detroit 11 D6
Dhaka 22 D5
DJIBOUTI 27 B8
Dodoma 27 D7
Doha 22 D3
DOMINICA 11 F8
   *capital* Roseau
DOMINICAN REPUBLIC 11 E8
Dublin 18 C4
Dushanbe 22 C4

## E

ECUADOR 14 A3
EGYPT 27 A6
El Aaiun 26 A3
EL SALVADOR 11 D9
Elbrus, Mount 21 E8
English Channel 18 C5
EQUATORIAL GUINEA
   26 D4
Erebus, Mount 34 E5
ERITREA 27 B7
ESTONIA 19 C7
ETHIOPIA 27 C7
Everest, Mount 24 D5

## F

Faeroe Islands 18 B5
Falkland Islands 15 C9
Fiji 31 C7
FINLAND 19 B7
FRANCE 18 D5
Freetown 26 C3
French Guiana 14 D3
French Polynesia 31 C10

## G

GABON 26 D5
Gaborone 27 E6
GAMBIA 26 B2
Ganges River 22 D4–5
Georgetown 14 D2
GEORGIA 22 B3
GERMANY 19 D6
GHANA 26 C4
Gibraltar 18 F4
Gibraltar, Strait of 18 F3
Gobi Desert 24 D5
Grand Canyon 13 B7–C7
Great Barrier Reef 32 C5
Great Dividing Range
   30 D5
Great Lakes 13 D6
GREECE 19 E7–F7
Greenland 10 D3, 35 A8
GRENADA 11 F8
   *capital* Saint George's
Guadalajara 11 B8
Guadeloupe 11 F8
GUATEMALA 11 C8
Guatemala City 11 C8
GUINEA 26 C3
GUINEA-BISSAU 26 C2
GUYANA 14 C2–D2

## H

HAITI 11 E8
Hanoi 23 E6
Harare 27 E6
Harbin 23 C7
Havana 11 D8
Hawaii 11 A6
Helsinki 19 B7
Himalayas 24 D5
HONDURAS 11 D8
Hong Kong 23 D7

Honiara 31 B6
Huang He River 23 D6
Hudson Bay 10 D5, 12 D5
HUNGARY 19 D6

## I

ICELAND 18 A4
INDIA 22 D4–E4
INDONESIA 23 F6
Indus River 22 D4, 24 D4
IRAN 22 C3–D3
IRAQ 22 C3
IRELAND 18 C4
Irian Jaya 23 F8
Irish Sea 18 C4
ISRAEL 22 C2
Istanbul 19 E8
ITALY 19 E6

## J

Jakarta 23 F6
JAMAICA 11 E8
JAPAN 23 C7
Java 25 F6–7
Jerusalem 22 C2
Johannesburg 27 F6
JORDAN 22 C2

## K

Kabul 22 D4
Kalahari Desert 29 F6
Kaliningrad 19 C7
Kampala 27 C7
Karachi 22 D4
Kathmandu 22 D5
KAZAKHSTAN 22 C4
KENYA 27 C7
Kermadec Islands 31 D7
Khartoum 27 B6
Kiev 19 D8
Kigali 27 D6
Kilimanjaro, Mount 29 D7
Kingston 11 E8
Kinshasa 26 D5
KIRIBATI 31 B8
   *capital* Tarawa
Kuala Lumpur 23 F6
KUWAIT 22 C3
Kuwait City 22 C3
KYRGYZSTAN 22 C4

## L

La Paz 14 C5
Lagos 26 C4
LAOS 23 E6
LATVIA 19 C7
LEBANON 22 C3
LESOTHO 27 F6
LIBERIA 26 C3
Libreville 26 C5
LIBYA 26 A5
LIECHTENSTEIN 19 D6
   *capital* Vaduz
Lilongwe 27 E7
Lima 14 A4